THE WAY OF THE
BODYGUARD

Library of Congress Cataloging-in-Publication Data

The Way of the Bodyguard / Nick Spill. – 1st U.S. edition
How to be a bodyguard
Knowledge not gossip
For bodyguards, past, present and future

ISBN 978-0-9839080-5-0 Print edition

1. Bodyguards - non-fiction. 2. Advice and How to – non-fiction. 3.
Philosophy – non-fiction. 4. Religion and Spirituality – Eastern Philosophy
– non-fiction. 5. True Accounts – non-fiction.

Book Design: www.52novels.com

Cover Damonza

Cover Photo by Leon Smith Photography

DISCLAIMER: Some names and identifying details have been changed or
omitted to protect the privacy of individuals.

More information about Nick Spill is available on:
http://nickspill.com

http://nickspill.blogspot.com/

http://wayofthebodyguard.com

Praise from professional bodyguards and investigators

"The book should serve for coming generations as the BIBLE. For classic bodyguard operatives. As the founder and CEO of ISA –ISRAEL, I recommend it to all our students."

Mirza David, International Security Academy, Israel.

"Every bodyguard and protection specialist should read this. This is essential reading. I insist all my bodyguards teams read a copy."

Joe Biundini, President FAM International.

"The Way of the Bodyguard is a great example of how its done right. Nick shares some real life experiences that will keep you on your toes, a must read!"

Adam Hamon, President, Regiment Security LLC and co-host of Outdoor Channel's Elite Tactical Unit.

"Nick Spill paints a vivid picture of what it is like to be a bodyguard with plenty of realism and excitement, though its not always glamorous. He lets you know how you can become one and what it takes to be a bodyguard. A fascinating read, not to be missed."

Laura Lanfield, author of Bail Bonds Babylon, private investigator and bail bondsman for over 30 years.

"The author has done a fine job describing the highs and lows of bodyguarding. The writing is clear and entertaining, and the information is right on. Take it from a guy who has guarded presidents, presidential candidates, religious leaders, and high-profile criminals, this book is a must read for anyone interested in the field."

Loren Christensen, Masters Hall of Fame in 2011, author of countless nonfiction books including with Lt. Col. Dave Grossman the groundbreaking must read 'On Combat' and his new best selling Fiction series 'Dukkha.'

"This book is a must read because it's not sex, murder, mayhem, or trivial stories about being a 'bodyguard'. It's a conceptual book about the way (the Tao) of being a bodyguard. If there ever was a manual of the correct way to understand a bodyguard's real perspective and ones ability to be a body guard this book by Nick Spill is it."

Bram Frank , Grandmaster Conceptual Modern Arnis / Tactical Arms, Modern Arnis Grandmaster and author of Conceptual Modern Arnis and WHFSC Grandmasters Compendium Vol #1 & #2.

Contents

THE WAY OF THE
BODYGUARD

HOW TO BE A BODYGUARD

FOR BODYGUARDS PAST, PRESENT AND FUTURE

Nick Spill

Prologue

My First Bodyguard Job

Nathan waved his hand to get the teacher's attention. His knees shook under his desk, sweat poured off his acne-cratered forehead and down his nose. Nathan desperately wanted to go to the bathroom. He pleaded.

The new teacher, a young woman with thin lips and a red cardigan had told him he could not go. We were half way through a written test. I sat next to Nathan and glared at her.

I watched Nathan lose control. A dark stain filled his pants and his pee dripped to the schoolroom floor. He started to sob quietly. He looked humiliated and ashamed. I was angry. I could not protect my friend.

After class, some of the boys tried to bully Nathan but I hit the biggest kid and they backed down.

The next day Nathan brought girlie magazines to school. The naked women wore black stockings and garter belts. I rented out the magazines for 10 pence to boys who looked at them in the stalls. I also made sure no one touched Nathan. We split the profits. Nathan was my client.

I did not realize that this was my first bodyguard job. I was 11 years old.

It took me a long time to understand that my profession was to be a bodyguard, to protect people.

Introduction

Eluding the Paparazzi

I carried her in my arms as I ran along the beach in darkness. I raised my knees up so I would not trip on the sand. We looked like a parody of the cover from Kevin Costner's film, "The Bodyguard." The young woman had already thrown up and was now drooling over my black shirt. She was so stoned she did not seem to mind being bounced around. I held her close to me, carefully.

Somewhere behind us in the dark, paparazzi were chasing us. We had eluded the crowds who were waiting outside the Collins Avenue hotel and the side entrances. We had slipped out the back, onto the beach and were making a dash for her hotel a few long blocks north.

The other bodyguard called ahead to security at her hotel. A large man dressed in black opened the hidden beach access gate so we could slip inside the property. His face was expressionless.

The young woman in my arms was at the time the most famous person in the world. She was on Miami Beach to star in a film. The wake up call was scheduled for 8 AM. It was now well after 6 A.M.

She woke up as we passed the swimming pool and mumbled that she wanted to swim. This had happened the previous night and we had had to watch her cavort naked in the pool before we managed to fish her out. I kept hold of her as we raced to her room. We took the stairs so we would not meet any of the other guests in the elevator with cell phone cameras.

The stench in her room was unbearable. Three tiny dogs had been locked up since four in the afternoon. There was dog poop and piddle on the floor and carpets. I placed her on her bed and made sure she would not throw up or do anything unpleasant in the bed. I covered her up and turned off the lights. She had passed out. She was safe, for now. Someone else would wake her up and walk the dogs.

The week before I had received a call from a business associate in Australia who needed another bodyguard to look after some celebrity in Miami. We had met at a bodyguard school reunion in Las Vegas and had forged a bond. We both liked to be low key and stay in the background. His partner had been traveling with this celebrity non-stop for several weeks and needed an extra hand while they were on Miami Beach. The day rate was low and there was no guaranteed 12-hour shift, as the hours would be flexible. Would I be interested?

The bodyguard I had worked with the last few days was just as low key. At some private parties and closed events, even other security people thought she was unprotected. But we were nearby, watching and could move in, if needed.

The most stressful part of any bodyguard work is usually logistics. This is not a code word for catching a bullet. Bodyguards have been called bullet catchers, as they would take a bullet for their client, or throw themselves in harm's way to protect their Protectee. (Technical note: we protect the Protectee or the principal. He or she can be the client or the client can hire us to protect someone else, whom we call the Protectee). Our mission is usually more mundane, like getting the Protectee from point A to point B, on time, unscathed and unflustered. Our biggest enemies are usually time and distance.

On this endless bodyguard detail, (a detail, to put it simply, is a job that employs a team of protection agents) the other bodyguard briefed me about times, places, people involved, what our schedule looked like, at least at the start of our shift. What the celebrity expects from us. How we are to act around her. Celebrities do want their photos taken, as long as they look good and you stay out of the photo. There is an art to this kind of bodyguard positioning, how you place yourself in relation to the celebrity and where you are not obviously in the picture but nearby and protecting the celebrity from photographers, media people, hangers on and the overenthusiastic crowds and stalkers. Every celebrity has a different idea of what you should be doing and how you should look. These ideas are sometimes not very sophisticated or sensible. So these sorts of bodyguard details are always learn as you go. Then there are the stalkers. You are not famous until you have at least one stalker. Some of them are quiet, clever and maniacal. Then there is the reluctance of the celebrity to inform us about her itinerary and any secret agendas. Well, they are secret. Like a boyfriend or girlfriend no one is supposed to know about. Or drug or alcohol use. What should not end up in the media or on the Internet.

Another shift had finally ended and I was off to bed at 8 in the morning. Our official start time for the next day was 2 PM, although it was already the next day.

Days turned to weeks but the detail finally ended. I added up the hours I had worked and what I had earned. I had to do some hard thinking. Was it worth it? As you will find out as a bodyguard, experience can be expensive. There were issues to think about. This is an extreme version of the type of bodyguard detail you think you want. Once inside the protective bubble, once living this life, you realize it's not that good a deal. No wonder she goes through bodyguards and bodyguard agencies so quickly. Living such an exposed life where you are under such scrutiny, media exposure and pressure to perform for the public but still maintain some dignity and privacy, can be daunting. For a bodyguard, it can be overwhelming.

The list of features in such jobs can be exhausting. First, there are the long days, which usually ran to 18 hours. This in itself is what you signed up for is it not? Long hours go with the profession. But there was no money for food or other expenses. Many similar security details incorporate a daily allowance for food and drink and incidentals. It might be a small amount but over the days and weeks, it mounts up. Daily expense allowances are a way of showing respect to your bodyguards. You look after your bodyguards and do not treat them like, what is the word that comes to mind? Dirt? Cattle? Slaves?

Then there was no tip money to spread around to get other people to help you. Now I need to explain this. Usually if we go into a restaurant or a club or anywhere where you would usually pay, you tip the help. I am not talking about a dollar here, a fiver there; I am talking about twenty to hundred dollar bills. Better service goes with larger tips. The other workers you interact with make their living off tips. They probably think you are earning enormous amounts of money as "her bodyguard" and expect a little extra for giving her better attention and service. But if you are a famous person, and carry no cash or credit cards, expect everything for free and get paid huge amounts of money just for showing up at a party or a night club and everybody is vying to dress you, give you free make up, hair extensions, shoes and so on, why would you dream of tipping anyone?

I took the assignment as a learning experience. I never want to do extended runs with that type of person again. I became more discerning about whom I protected. But that is all part of being a bodyguard. You get great jobs and you get interesting jobs. My philosophy was that long as I got paid and the client was safe and happy, it was all good. There are great clients, great Protectees who look after their bodyguards, pay them well and respect them. However, bodyguards tend to stay in these types of bodyguard details. It can be rare to acquire a position with such Protectees, despite the long hours, grueling travel schedules, and long periods away from home. There are bodyguard details like that out there. And if you land in one, you would be wise to stay and count your blessings. For every great bodyguard job, however challenging, there are several that are not so pleasant. Then there are the long hours of waiting, of doing nothing, of standing or sitting, wondering what are you doing with your life in such a tedious profession? Where is the excitement?

Which brings me to the central question, why do you want to be a bodyguard? Why would you spend long hours waiting around doing nothing and expecting the very worst thing to happen to you? So that we are clear, the very worst thing is dying.

Why choose this profession?

You have trained for years in martial arts, firearms, verbal judo, and new languages. You have invested in the latest equipment, expensive clothes and shoes. You have a background in Special Forces or other specialist activities and have done stuff you cannot even tell your dog about, if you had a dog, but you have no pets, because you are never home. You are in incredible shape, you workout every day.

Now you are on your first bodyguard assignment, stuck in a hotel corridor. It looks like you will be standing by a door for your entire 12-hour shift. Your radio does not work, nor do you have cell phone service. You are unsure what your mission is and you need to go to the bathroom, urgently.

Welcome to the life of a bodyguard; under briefed, under-paid, overextended and in situations you have no control over and, beyond bored. We will return to the hotel corridor later but why another book about bodyguards? And why do you want to be one?

Is it the Romance or the Thrill of Action?

A search on Amazon.com reveals there are more romance books on bodyguards than manuals or textbooks on the profession. This book is far from romantic. My book is different. I am in the business. This is not a dry how to guide nor is it a technical manual. There are plenty of good manuals out there that cover the basics of being a bodyguard. The romance comes later when you can tell stories about what you did and your memory becomes sweeter when you forget all the long boring days you endured.

Why another book on Bodyguards?

This book is called "The Way of the Bodyguard" because becoming a bodyguard entails a long journey, a state of mind and a way of life. You never quite reach your destination, you are always learning, and the job defines your existence. You are a protector by nature.

Being a bodyguard is an extraordinary commitment, unlike any other profession, even law enforcement, for the simple reason you might have to give up your life to save your client.

It is a state of mind, because once you have been trained to see the World in a certain way you can never escape your training; how you exit a car, how you enter a room, how you position yourself in a space, how you look after and think of your loved ones. There are a thousand behaviors that protect and influence how you live your life, serve others and protect those closest to you. The Way, is a positive and protective means to a richer and safer life. It is living without fear.

If you are in the news you are probably dead, and if you are reading about yourself, you are definitely in trouble.

Am I being overly dramatic? Conduct a simple search engine inquiry for "bodyguard" in the news category. What do you find? Dead bodyguards, bodyguards in trouble, bodyguards in disgrace. You very rarely read about bodyguards who saved someone or prevented something bad from happening. If there is a positive news story, it's probably manufactured! When you are in the news you are history, in court or in the ground. And if you are not history, you do not write a tell-all book. That would mean you would be out of the business, no one would ever hire you again. Clients want discretion and protection, not revelation and sensation.

Protectees do not want to read about their own bodyguards. They want to read about themselves, not their protectors. If you gain publicity, or you talk about your Protectee to the press, you are unemployed. Trust and loyalty are key to the bodyguard Protectee relationship.

One of the reasons a celebrity can hire you is to ensure that the paparazzi do not obtain that delicious drunk out of her mind half undressed shot that will haunt her career for the rest of her life. The sort of photos that spread through the Internet like a virus and stay forever.

In the bodyguard business, discretion is key. For if you tell, no one will hire you. Although in this strange celebrity obsessed world, logic and common sense do not always triumph. I am sure if I told some really bizarre true stories I would procure more bodyguard details, but from people I would not want to protect.

There is Felony Stupid then Bodyguard Stupid and then Celebrity Stupid. If you can combine all three Stupids, you have a volatile mix, Felony Bodyguard Celebrity Stupid. We want to avoid all such Stupids. Every bodyguard who has been in the business for a long time has stories about such people.

The Way is the Code

As a bodyguard you have to live by your code and it is not a vague set of guidelines, it's a code. I can only live by my code. I call it the Way of the Bodyguard and if I am hired, I will keep quiet.

Confidentiality, discretion and the Law

Most States have laws concerning client confidentiality. Under Florida Statute Chapter 493, revealing the client's name and any information about a case without the client's permission is a misdemeanor. Violators can be fined up to $5,000 and lose their license for 5 years. The private investigator or bodyguard cannot even tell a Law Enforcement officer who the client is, unless the client agrees.

One bodyguard I know has been dragged out of his car and handcuffed in several different jurisdictions, because he would not tell the local patrol officer who pulled up on him why he was parked outside an expensive house in an exclusive neighborhood. Both parties might have taken their respective roles to extremes, but a visit by the sergeant got my friend unhandcuffed, with an apology and a lesson to the arresting officer in Chapter 493. Of course telling the officer that his department was going to be sued and the bodyguard would own the police department for such a wrongful arrest hardly endeared the bodyguard to the officer, who was only doing his job, if slightly uninformed about a Statute that would no longer be obscure to him.

A little charm, a sincere smile and some common sense goes a long way in defusing and deflecting such small incidents. Most officers have good street instincts about who is a good guy and who is a bad guy. It is wise not to confuse these supposed street instincts by acting like an asshole. Such incidents can be blown out of proportion so easily and make a bodyguard's life more difficult than it already is.

You do not talk about your clients, period.

Beyond or Behind the Law

Then there are other dynamics that enter into the situation when dealing with local Law Enforcement. In some States, police officers can work privately as bodyguards, while off duty of course. This can add to the confusion and competition as to who can work where, for how much, and with whom. Private bodyguard agencies that work in other States hire off duty cops. It is called local assurance, having a local badge to help out if something goes wrong. If you are operating in territory that is not your own or is unfamiliar, it is good to have local cops as your protection. Which answers in some small way the question, who is protecting the protectors? Traveling outside the U.S.A. also necessitates using local law enforcement, whether in Mexico or Nigeria or anywhere. If you have a bodyguard team, it is wise to have that local assurance, someone who can make a call or flash a badge or rack an AK-47 when absolutely needed.

It's your Life

Back to losing your life in your new profession. It's all the same for you anyway. If you lose your client, you do not have a career. No one would hire you if you got your Protectee killed.

One bodyguard school I attended began with the taciturn instructor informing the class that if they were not prepared to die for their client they should walk out right away. They would get their money back. The person who had arranged the school and had all the money in his pocket was shitting himself in the back of the room, but no one left. Why? Not because we have a big ego and don't want to show the rest of the class that we are cowards. But because we never qualify for this position, dead bodyguard, until it is too late. Look at news stories in search engines, the bodyguard is shot first.

There was another lesson to this story I learned much later. Bodyguarding is a business, and not as I so horribly put it, a verb masquerading as a noun. The bodyguard with all the money in his pocket at the end wins. Bodyguards are replaceable. There is always somebody better qualified (in the client's mind at least) who can do the job cheaper.

No room for egos

This is a not a kiss and tell book nor a punch and brag book. There are other books out there written by large egos. Nothing wrong with a super sized ego if it works for you and a few such big egos have made a name for themselves in the movie and rock and roll protection business, where they have to deal with even bigger egos, their Protectees.

Sometimes it takes a big ego to handle an even bigger and crazier ego. "Tell all" bodyguard books can be entertaining to read but will not teach much other than if you are a giant crazy bad ass you can fantasize about being God's gift to rock and roll bodyguards. If you feel, notice I do not use the word "think" here, as think is not the correct verb, if you feel that is the life for you, then this book, this Way, is not for you.

A huge ego is a definite hindrance to being a good bodyguard. That is why for most details I like to hire guys older than 35, and who don't live with their mother. There is a good story there, read it later on.

The mature bodyguard has been around the block a few times, not necessarily on his feet and he has had enough experience to know what to do and more importantly what not to do. He has nothing to prove other than he is a professional.

Over 35 years old might appear arbitrary but I will not hire anyone under 21, again. The worst under 21 story I can imagine did come true.

I did hire a man, a boy, from another agency in South Florida. Everyone was supposed to be over 21. I did not know, back then, you could apply for a Statewide Firearms License, a G License if you were under 21. You cannot obtain a concealed weapons license if you are under 21. The boy was a little strange, looked too young and kept to himself. He was covering the back door of a large property we were managing that day and he stayed out of trouble. He did not respond to radio calls, so I wondered what he was doing. I had 20 other men I had never worked with either, to worry about. It was another endless shift but nothing went wrong, we had a lot of security, a strong presence and the client was happy. I made a mental note to not hire this kid again.

I saw him a few months later when he was looking after a very beautiful and frightened young lady who had been threatened by her ex-boss. I was taking the 12 hour day shift. I stayed outside in my car where I had a full view of the property, as were my instructions. When I came to replace the young bodyguard the next day, he was inside and it did not look like he had been using the sofa in the living room to sit on that night. I had no definitive proof of what I thought had happened, so I kept quiet. It was not my contract. I was just helping out a colleague in another agency.

The next time I heard about him, he had murdered four people in cold blood. Whatever happened to vetting? How could this other security company have hired him? He was 23 years old when I wrote this, and serving 5 life sentences plus 75 years.

It sounds glib to say that sometimes you just have to hire who is available. But for long-term bodyguard details, it is best to hire more experienced men and women, who are mature and in shape. Even then you can make mistakes. After Hurricane Katrina hit New Orleans, there were a large number of security personnel swarming into Louisiana. Reputable security companies had lucrative contracts that needed immediate staffing. Men were hired who should not own a gun, let alone carry one on duty. I found this out the hard way when we accidentally hired one of these clowns in a very large bodyguard detail on the West Coast. We eventually fired him after receiving information about what he had done in New Orleans, so the vetting process did work, if a little slowly. His "Way" was the highway not our hotel corridors.

The Way of the Bodyguard is not a first nor for many, a second career. It is a natural continuation of your development as a full human being with elite protection skills and other mature qualities. You feel good about yourself, confident but not cocky. You are always ready to learn, as you are open to new ideas, new training. You love to protect people and have a natural affinity to safeguard those around you. You are a protector.

Adults Only

Why would I hire some young guy who wants to prove himself? If you want to prove yourself, join the Armed Forces, go and fight the Global War on Terrorism or whatever it is called now. Don't try and be a bodyguard. No one is interested in your ego. I say all the time to new employees and new bodyguards: It's not about you; it's about the Protectee. No one cares about you. It's the Protectee who counts. You are just there to protect and serve. Stop whining and start listening. Well, it's usually never that drastic but you get my point.

Being a bodyguard can be a very humbling experience. Protectees can treat their bodyguards like garbage. Bodyguards might have to take out the garbage, although this can be turned into an opportunity to execute some counter surveillance, but we will get to that later. Men who say, "Oh, I cannot carry the dry cleaning! I have to be in a secure posture at all times!" will certainly assume the position. There are times when you have to do tasks to make the Protectee happy, but not what you are thinking. That would be a foolish.

A Bodyguard with Benefits

Sleeping with your Protectee or client is a fatal mistake. It might seem inevitable or a good idea at the time but these relationships do not last. If you have read any Bodyguard Romances, well, you get the picture. In real life, such relationships undermine the safety of your Protectee.

Having any kind of sexual relationship with your Protectee usually leads to disaster. Even if the disaster is just being fired. I had a handsome young man who was sleeping with a real life Princess. She took him to Paris. He was her bodyguard for a year. He got paid very well. I never verified the amount of the tips. But the rumor was she tipped very well. He will not be hired by anyone connected to that Princess again but he will always have Paris.

Another bodyguard who worked for me did not survive his initial interview. The client, who was the Protectee, was lying in bed in a seductive outfit. There were a lot of mirrors in the bedroom and they were not for adjusting her hair. A large black and white photograph was displayed prominently. The prospective bodyguard could not make out the image. He looked deeper and realized it was a blown up X-ray of someone's middle region and a large rocket shaped instrument was embedded in the largest open cavity.

"Do you like what you see?" She purred. For once in his life, he was stumped for words. He did not take the job. When the attractive heiress died a few years later, she left millions of dollars in her will to her bodyguards and her pet dogs.

There are happy endings. There are exceptions. The richest woman in Israel married her bodyguard. Patty Hearst married her full time protector. Princess Stephanie of Monaco married her bodyguard, if only for 15 months. The list is short, but as a rule, the Way of the Bodyguard does not incorporate physical intimacy with the people you are paid to protect.

While we are on the subject of intimacy, I have never taken a photograph with a celebrity or other famous person I have protected. I am not shy, I love taking photographs and am obsessive about documenting events, but acquiring trophy photographs is unprofessional. The act is also destabilizing, even in a private situation and infringes on the Protectee's sense of privacy. People we protect are always saying yes, because they are usually popular and need public approval and acclaim, and do not as a rule say no to their bodyguards wanting photographs with them. Plain and simple, it is just unprofessional. And if anyone I hire makes a habit of doing this, I see the act as indicative of other undesirable traits; that the bodyguard is more concerned with himself and his self image than that of the person he is supposed to be protecting.

I have had embarrassing situations where other bodyguards have asked for photographs and posed with the people they are supposed to be protecting. Such situations have been out of my control and I did not want to make the officer or bodyguard look stupid. It is so easy to make quick enemies in this business of sensitive egos. But looking back I have no photographs of anyone I protected. And I am quite happy about that. My mission was not to collect photos or autographs but to protect. Displaying photos taken with celebrities can appear as good marketing, especially to people who know little about bodyguard work.

So you should not be a bodyguard with benefits. But you can keep the Protectee happy, as in paying attention to fine points, such as walking the dog.

What is wrong with walking the dog outside the secured property? You have an opportunity to assert your Alpha personality over the dog, and you become acquainted with the neighborhood at night, at a different time. You can keep in contact with your Protectee's property, never leaving sight of it and you get to sniff the fresh air, like your new pal. Dogs have been used as protective animals for centuries, even little dogs, well maybe not mindless teacup puppies smaller than baby rats. You can turn what might seem an inappropriate task into one that can benefit your immediate and long-term aims; guarding the Protectee and training the dog to obey you.

The question you have to ask yourself is, why do you want to be a bodyguard?

Do you think it is glamorous? Exciting? Action packed? Do you think the ladies, or men, will be attracted to you if you say you are a professional bodyguard? Do you think you will make huge amounts of money? Make love to beautiful women who are attracted to dangerous men? Have wild drunken parties with your mates? Impress men who thought you were not tough enough?

If you want to be a bodyguard for those macho or romantic reasons, they are the wrong reasons.

Your motivation has to be something else entirely. You have to be committed to the Way and for me to explain that to you, you will have to read on.

The Difference between Personal Security Detail (PSD) work and civilian bodyguard work

Lets clear something up here as you have read how much some men are making over in the sandbox. Yes, you used to be able to clear huge amounts, over $1,000 a day in Iraq, Afghanistan or other hot places. Why? It is extremely dangerous. As part of a Personal Security Detail (PSD) team you carry long guns, lots of ammo, a handgun and medical kit plus tons of other equipment. Such open carry also assumes a different set of rules of engagement. These rules of engagement are coming under closer scrutiny. High profile and high risk equals high pay because the market can handle such pay rates from $600 to $1,000 a day. Although now pay rates are going down in such high risk areas in the Middle East, Africa and Afghanistan and more companies are hiring cheaper and tougher East Europeans and Russians, who eat, complain and consume less and do not need expensive air conditioning and hot showers. Remember there is always someone cheaper and supposedly better qualified who can replace your PSD or bodyguard detail.

The goal of this book is not to become a PSD operator but a bodyguard in a civilian job. Think nice hotel rooms rather than tents and air-conditioned containers with bunks. To become a PSD operator, if you have the correct qualifications, is, in a sense easier. You have your DD214, (Department of Defense's record of separation from Military service that verifies what you did and when), physical fitness, some protection or PSD training experience and there is a vast online set of resources and networks for such jobs.

The toughest Snake Eater does not a good Bodyguard make

You can be a highly skilled PSD operator and make a lousy civilian bodyguard. You can be the toughest snake eater and Special Forces operator and not have the manners or civilian grace to be a tame bodyguard. I have encountered many fresh out of the sandbox operators who might have been brilliant at what they were doing over there in such an extreme environment, with different verbal and shoot don't shoot skills, but back here in the U.S.A is a different matter.

In the so-called civilized world, they have been too highstrung and too nervous and they have lacked the cool grace to put civilian and corporate Protectees at ease. As a PSD operator, you are usually in a team of men from similar backgrounds with matching and complimentary skill sets. You are all in the same sandbox together. There is or should be a camaraderie and team spirit amongst certain specific groups of operators that you do not achieve in the civilian bodyguard world.

For PSD work, risk equals reward. And risk can equal bad luck. Riding shotgun in a large convoy, heavily and openly armed, where you figuratively have a sign over the convoy announcing, "Bomb me! I'm an American!" is vastly different from riding in a chase car behind a limo in an American city, dressed in a suit, carrying concealed. You can be highly skilled and work with an incredible PSD team, but still get unlucky from one I.E.D. (improvised explosive device) that just happens to have your name on it. This can have nothing to do with your skills and experience. You can be the toughest baddest snake eater Special Forces veteran with unmatched firearms skills, the coolest tattoos, and still be killed from no tactical fault of your own. This tragedy has happened to far too many highly skilled operators, men who were the baddest, meanest snake eaters. All it took was one I.E.D. to obliterate them.

A Close Protection officer Stateside, or bodyguard, if he does carry a firearm, carries it concealed and conforms to the local laws regarding use of deadly force. As a civilian, you are treated no differently than any other person. You are not Law Enforcement and in most States, have no powers of arrest or other legal powers. Day rates can be a lot less too. The market in the U.S. can dictate lower rates and different States with their licensing requirements can create their own dynamics with regards to supply and demand.

Only NYPD officers and retired cops could carry in New York City before H.R. 218. They had, and for all intents and purposes still have, a captive market for armed security. A highly trained private investigator from Florida cannot carry a firearm in New York City (unless he qualifies as an ex Cop under H.R. 218).

In the U.S. rates can vary on average from $250 to $500 a day, if you are lucky. Elsewhere, because of intense competition, unscrupulous practices of other agencies and unlicensed bodyguards, prices can be even lower. There are many types of bodyguard jobs. The best though are high paying Executive Protection details where you are employed on a full time basis to provide protection and security consulting for a large corporation or an affluent and sane family. I am not joking about the "sane" qualifier. If you have worked for some very wealthy families you will know what I am talking about.

Do you really really want to be a bodyguard?

I am still trying to dissuade you from being a bodyguard. The pay can be low (for the risks you take) and erratic. The work can be boring, conditions can be unpleasant and the company you keep, not to mention the clients, can be questionable.

But let's skip the training, and all the thousands and thousands of dollars you have spent to qualify as a bodyguard and how you sold your soul to win that difficult, elusive first job. Let's go straight to the first day of your new career.

The First Day

You arrive at your first job. You enter the Command Post (CP), a converted room in a prestigious hotel downtown. (You have already valet parked your car and are down at least half a days pay for the privilege of using their valet). There is no activity in the CP, but the one man behind a desk appears bored and not pleased to see you. He does not know who you are, and you fail to make a good first impression. (Now there is an entire section on that - making the first and lasting impression.) So, without any pleasant conversation, he tells you to immediately go to a hotel room and stand outside. Do not knock. Wait. You are given a radio but no other instructions. There is the assumption that the Protectee is inside the room. You hope. That's all. You go to that hotel floor, arrive at the room and then what?

You check the radio. Is it on the right frequency? No one gave you a communications card or radio codes or anything. You try a radio check but it does not work on that floor. You try your cell phone and call the CP. The call fails - no signal. Now what do you do? You have no idea who the Protectee is - you assume it's a male but on listening at the door you do not hear anything. There is a Do Not Disturb sign on the door. Is that a good sign or a bad sign?

So you are a recent graduate from a top rated Executive Protection Specialist School. You have invested thousands of dollars on training for your new profession. You have the makings of a great looking resume, which does not seem to matter right now because:

1. You do not know and would not recognize your Protectee. Is there only one person in the suite? Is this the right exit the Protectee would take? Does he know whom you are and what you are supposed to do? Do you?

2. Your communications do not work. You are in a hotel dead zone.

3. You do not know what exactly you should do next.

4. The second cup of coffee is starting to work, too well, and you want to go to the bathroom but you cannot leave your post, even for a minute.

5. Two hours pass and it feels like an entire day. There is no maid on the floor yet, no activity at all and now you are hungry. Why didn't you pack a granola bar or something in your suit jacket pocket? Why didn't they teach you that at the Expensive Executive Protection School you attended? And lets not forget about 6!

6. You forgot to ask about parking, who is paying for your car to be valet parked and can you charge it to a room?

7. Perhaps you should have attended that 10 day High Risk PSD training course. Instead of standing in a Five Star hotel you could be running around in a hot inhospitable country wearing 80 pounds of gear and a cool tricked out M-4 with 8 spare magazines and be part of a great PSD Team. The street you are roaring down in your armored trucks has gone strangely quiet. All the pedestrians and other traffic have disappeared. You are passing an abandoned car that was not there the day before. Your life flashes before your eyes. Maybe that route was not such a good idea. The civilian route was smarter, if not so well paid, in the short term.

Does that situation sound familiar? The hotel corridor, not the I.E.D. about to explode. Have you ever been in a place where everything is stacked against you? You have not been given enough information to do your job and you don't have enough experience to ask the right questions. Other people working with you, who don't care if you fail, assume you know what you are doing. This is a banal example but more representative of our work situation than bizarre and overly dramatic Hollywood movie depictions of bodyguards.

Staying at a 5 star hotel in Beverly Hills, we hired a new bodyguard for a Saudi princess. He was an active duty LAPD detective, and looked like Mexican Pete with a droopy mustache and a potbelly. He was not badly dressed, his sports coat and tie matched his looks, not exactly film star elegant to say the least. He probably is a good detective, but left something to be desired in the first impressions count in the bodyguard department, especially with Saudis who are so conscious of how they appear and how their bodyguards should look the part. We told Mexican Pete to stand outside a hotel door and follow the Princess. He had no idea what she looked like. Like a Saudi princess of course, not like one of her ladies in waiting, of whom there were three, and not like her sister, of whom there was only one, and whom looked exactly like her princess sister, especially if you were seeing her for the first time and could not tell the finer points that set the princess apart from her sister or her three ladies in waiting. Hint: the princess had a more expensive watch, a more luxurious necklace.

When the princess came out of her room to go downstairs for a late afternoon shopping spree, he never got a chance to introduce himself, not that he was allowed to talk to her, not that he recognized her. We found out later she took one look at him and did not like him. She did not let him into the elevator with her and her three ladies in waiting. She did not let him get in the SUV with her, where he should have positioned himself next to the driver. She ignored him. And that was his entire experience with our team of 20 plus bodyguards at that hotel. At least he had a full time paying job to go back to. He failed for no other reason than he did not look the part. Come to think of it, his stomach was a little on the extended side.

"Who was that man outside the door?" She asked me later. "He looked so ugly. Not like you."

"Yes, we love your accent, where are you from?" Her sister asked as the elevator stopped at the first floor and I smiled politely.

"Miami."

"Oh no. Not with that cute accent. You are kidding."

There are many stories like that. Bodyguards who do not make the first hour let alone first day because of something they did or did not do or how they looked.

I came back to a five star hotel in a particular West Coast city to find in my two-day absence, my number two man had hired someone I would never have hired. There was just something about him I did not like. Yes, it can be a fickle business and I could not be bothered finding out what that "something" was. The moment a particular Saudi princess saw him; she fired him on the spot. The princess exclaimed: "I don't like him. Go away!" He didn't last five minutes. I think this was the record on that endless detail. The poor guy, who actually did look film star handsome, was stuck with his valet parking bill. We were not going to pay it. And he never asked before hand where he should park, but more on that annoying little point later.

Welcome to the life of bodyguards. It is especially rough when you first start out. There are so many "tricks" you have to master, ways to think on your feet, to adapt and improvise, to overcome difficult situations. You have to think fast and be creative to survive in this profession. Like that hotel corridor situation.

Meanwhile back in the Corridor

This time, as your bladder is about to explode, you are in luck, as a room service waiter appears. You are friendly and do not act like a tough guy security jerk or whatever they call such men in the High Powered Elite and very Expensive Executive Protection Specialist School you graduated from. You talk to him respectfully and find out he is about to deliver breakfast on a trolley. You check the trolley and the order in the folder the waiter holds. Now you know the name of your Protectee and as you talk to the waiter, in hushed tones, you find out this is a standing order every day at this time, there is no one else in the room and he usually leaves his suite an hour after the delivery.

You knock on the door, announce room service, the Protectee opens the door, you catch a look at him as you introduce yourself and you let the waiter in. Your Protectee is in a dressing gown but at least he has seen you and now knows who you are. It happens very fast, very discreetly and friendly, you think. You did not shake your Protectee's hand because his dressing gown might have slipped open and besides he didn't look like he wanted to. You are his bodyguard not his buddy! You slip your new friend a nice tip, not knowing if you will be reimbursed but heck, its been three hours in your new profession and you want to ensure your success. (With that expensive valet parking charge as well, you are really in the hole!) That was one lesson you did learn at bodyguard school: make as many friends as possible in the hotel, friendliness and professional courtesy is appreciated but tipping is essential. You are just another worker.

Once the waiter disappears (happier and richer than you) down the corridor, you start to plan that run to the hotel staff toilet on the next floor the waiter has told you about. Or maybe you should try to radio the CP from another position on the floor while not leaving your post or line of sight of the suite door and request a 5-minute break now. And you can radio in that your Protectee is having breakfast in his room. Because you know if you do leave your post, that will be the time the team leader will come by to check you out and introduce himself to you. You want to make a good first impression, as you will never have a second chance.

When the detail leader does show up on your floor, you can now report with authority the situation, however banal. And you will look like you are in control and know what you are doing.

It is always the little things that can get you into trouble and out of trouble, just as quickly.

Lessons Learned

So what were the lessons learned here with the hotel corridor assignment? You need to plan everything out beforehand. Where do you park? Is it paid for? Do you have radios? Are there radio cards and comm rules? You know you need good field interview skills. Whether you call it tactical civility or being a good con artist, you have to think and talk fast on your feet. Being able to communicate with the room service waiter and getting vital information from him saved you. You also were considerate to him and acted respectfully and professionally. Now did you pick this up at the Bodyguard school? "The hotel staff is your best friends course." Or are you like this all the time? Also lay off the coffee, it's a diuretic and makes you pee. Being a bodyguard means you never get enough time to pee or do other stuff. Your time is not yours. So easy on the liquids and foods that might upset you. And pack a granola bar or two in your suit pocket.

Before you make a first impression

Those first fifteen seconds count

I receive calls all the time from a wide variety of young men who want to be bodyguards. The caller usually blows his chance in the first fifteen seconds. If you are making a cold call, then you only have a few seconds to capture the interest of the person on the other end of the phone.

Now I like to be conned, I like to be seduced, on the phone. What I mean is I like to observe the process by which someone can lure me into thinking and acting a certain way. It is a learning experience for me. How did he do that? What skills did he use? It happens so rarely, I have to be in the mood (you've heard that one before) and I appreciate the skill and finesse and energy someone transmits in placing that first call. If I receive a call from someone who is very good at communicating, can articulate what he wants and is very pleasing to listen to, I'll listen and help him, if I have the time. However, if he sounds tentative and unsure of himself, or sounds too cocky and demanding, I have no interest in talking to him. If he does not believe in what he is saying, why should I? If he cannot hook me in, how can he hook in others?

As a bodyguard you have to have "the gift of the gab," be able to talk to anyone and obtain results. You need to project confidence and sincerity, so that the person you are talking to believes in you and wants to help you. Charm is not enough, you need to be able to follow through so the person on the other side of that telephone does what you want. The same applies with face-to-face interactions.

If I receive a call from someone who projects no confidence, has neither telephone charm nor the ability to captivate on the phone, well, what can I say? Do you think you can gain these skills at a school? You can certainly work on them and try harder as I stated earlier, this guide is called the Way because it is a journey, and we are all learning, regardless of our skill levels. One segment of training you can never learn enough of and should be trained in the most, is verbal judo. It can be called tactical communications, word ninja, verbal karate, whatever the title, the effect is getting other people to do things that are going to help you and your Protectee.

Verbal Judo in other words

Verbal judo is not flipping over smart-ass phrases or tripping other people up on multi-syllable words. Verbal judo has been defined, written and taught by Dr. George Thompson, as the gentle art of persuasion, that redirects others behavior with words and generates voluntary compliance. You can redirect to the floor with some martial art technique or you can redirect behavior with verbal judo. Although every situation is different and as the saying goes, "ask twice then don't be nice."

The paperback Verbal Judo by Dr George Thompson, is mandatory reading for every cop and bodyguard. (See the Way of the Bodyguard Reading List at the end of the book.) Thompson emphasizes voluntary compliance through verbal skills but being a bodyguard puts you in a different situation. You do not have arrest powers, or a taser in your hand, so your persuasion skills have a different end game. More on this later.

Bodyguards have to have very good verbal skills, articulate in their needs and persuasive in their demands. You will see this material again.

So if you still want to follow the Way of the Bodyguard, where do you start? How do you break into the business?

Chapter One

How to Break into the Bodyguard Business

Where to start

Most men and women who want to break into the protection industry are former Law Enforcement, former Military or in a related Civilian profession; bouncer, martial artist, fitness trainer, or kindergarten teacher. The good news for those who are not ex-something is that you do not have to be a former cop or Special Forces warrior to become a bodyguard. Bodyguards come from all walks of life.

Recently, I attended a FBI SWAT demonstration and learned that only two had been patrol cops. The others were chemists, accountants and one of the SWAT leaders was a former bank loan officer. The head of the entire team had been a lobbyist. And I thought he was a Ranger. The same goes for bodyguards. We come from all walks of life. If you have the mindset and the ability to learn and operate in diverse challenging environments, there could be a place for you on a bodyguard team or working one on one with a Protectee. If you can keep ahead of 30 kindergarten kids for 6 hours a day, 5 days a week, maybe you have some of the skills needed to be a bodyguard!

Clients seem to think that cops or Special Forces operators make the best bodyguards and they gain a sense of false security from that impression. Sometimes a cop or a former Special Forces operator can be the least qualified person for a specific mission. We are talking about very specific training, skill sets, attitudes and experience for a competent bodyguard.

Some former "persons" might not have such skill sets, attitudes and experience.

Do not underestimate experience. If you are a SEAL you will be able to tap into a closed network of former SEALS who hire their own. You will come across warrior brethren networks all the time. Men work with other men who have had the same experiences and training. Marines want to work with other Marines. Rangers with other Rangers. Bouncers with other bouncers. Former Secret Service with other former Secret Service agents. They are comfortable with other men who have had the same type of training and reinforced mind sets, similar stressful experiences and who have triumphed or at least survived in their particular profession. No one wants to work with the FNG, the Frigging New Guy, the unknown, the untested. Would you? That's the problem. YOU are the FNG!

What to do first

Breaking into the business is difficult but not impossible. It is a Catch 22 situation. No one will hire you without experience, but you have no experience because no one will hire you.

As I mentioned in the Introduction, getting a position overseas in a high risk Personal Security Detail is vastly different. With your military experience and close quarter combat and proven shooting skills you can plug yourself into a closed but lucrative market for such PSD operators through various military service networks.

For a civilian bodyguard job, you need someone to vouch for your first position. Our work comes from personal recommendations, referrals, and networking. An experienced bodyguard with a good reputation can say, "Yes, I can vouch for him. He's a good guy, good operator." If you are good at what you do, keep your mouth shut when you are supposed to, show up on time, and are professional, word spreads. You will be hired again. It's that first time that can be difficult.

Here is where Special Forces retirees, Secret Service and FBI retirees have an advantage, they have a preexisting network of other retirees who have gone through the same situation and can recommend or know someone who can vouch for them for that hard to find first job. I am going to let you into a little secret, although I am going to catch flak for this. Some of these retirees know squat about bodyguard skills, are hopeless at protection work and think they know it all because of their previous Federal, State or local City employer and their elite retired status. Then there is the retiree who is brilliant, has all the right instincts and is humble and always willing to learn and do low paying jobs because he regards himself at the bottom of a new totem pole - so it is hopeless generalizing. There are all kinds in this business and remember you are dealing with guys who carry guns, have a high level of testosterone and might have to give up their lives or be hurt to protect their Protectee, so expect some unusual personalities. And that is probably the biggest understatement in this book.

Can you get a job from cold calling?

No. Only left out in the cold.

I used to get calls all the time from men who wanted to be bodyguards or thought they already were and wanted to be hired. I have no idea who they were, other than they could not read the instructions on my (former) web site. (Clue: being able to read instructions is rather critical to the job description).

As if after listening to them on the phone I would want to hire them or if I received their resume, with no cover letter, or maybe if I was lucky to receive a short note full of spelling mistakes, I would definitely want to hire them. It does not happen like that in this industry. Or rather it is rare to be hired over the phone from a cold call. I know there are exceptions and strangely enough in a new city with a large number of bodyguards to be hired in an impossibly short period, I have hired guys over the phone or rather told them to report to the Command Post (CP) to see if they are suitable. The nature of this business is such that the need for bodyguards can happen very quickly and can depend on being at the right place at the right time.

Timing is everything

I had been hanging out at a security company office when a call came in for a bodyguard for a long-term contract. The owner of the company turned to me and asked do you want it? It was easier for him to do that than make a bunch of phone calls. Of course I accepted. When dealing with other agencies, it is almost a golden rule that you never turn down a job offer. Because, if you decline, the agency might not call you first, the next time. Timing and networking are important.

That job lasted three months. I worked for an American gypsy family. I obtained a unique insider's look at gypsy life. As the only bodyguard and non-gypsy in many of their gatherings, it was a little disconcerting. Disconcerting as in "Hang on, if I'm the only non gypsy here and something goes wrong, who is going to be blamed, if I survive whatever it is that does go wrong?"

It was an education in a closed and secretive society that Federal Agencies had been trying to penetrate for years, at a huge cost in resources and manpower. The other bodyguard who worked the night shift recently took a vacation at the Federal Government's expense, for an unrelated crime, nothing to do with gypsies. And these same gypsies still operate today virtually untouched by Federal or State law enforcement.

The assignment gave rise to the question, how much do you want to be involved in protecting people whom you know very little about? Who speak another language? In this instance Romany, that no one else understands and who conduct various businesses right under your nose, of which you have very little knowledge?

I will deal with this later concerning client or Protectee selection. Who do you want to protect? And what risks are you willing to assume, provided of course they are legitimate Protectees?

Resumes help but rarely get you a job cold

The bodyguard business is a business like any other specialized profession. Take lawyers. To get hired by a law firm you are usually recruited out of Law School or later by a headhunter, if you are good or perceived to be good. There are ways that define excellence: Law Journal, great grades, and a stellar internship, a high-ranking Law School. You have an exemplary resume that matches the skills and expertise that the Law Firm wants and you undergo a series of elaborate interviews to acquire such a position.

It is the same in the bodyguard business. We do not usually have headhunters but we have bodyguard agencies that subcontract work and bodyguard schools that recommend graduates to potential openings. We have elaborate networks of bodyguards. It is a small world we work in. A high-ranking bodyguard school carries more prestige than a local 3-day school with a catchy web site but no real reputation. In the bodyguard business, if you mess up, word spreads fast. There was a list of men who came to New Orleans following the Katrina Hurricane, thinking they were the very best in personal protection. They were fired and now we know who they are. Getting a bad reputation is hard to live down.

A good resume is a start and a finish

Your resume can be important. The person who hires you wants to know what you have done but resumes alone do not get you jobs. And what goes into the resume will determine if it gets read in the first place. That is if you have anything of relevance to put in it. Being a warehouse manager for the last ten years does not impress a future hiring agency, nor does having seven unrelated positions in seven years. Having an elaborate Special Forces background and a sound DD214 looks good as does relevant training records and certifications that can be verified from reputable schools and sources.

A resume is really a window into what you have been doing professionally with your life, what training and awards or other accomplishments you have achieved. Most hiring Agencies can differentiate a solid honest resume from an inadequate and padded one immediately, having seen enough of them to last a lifetime.

Do not label your resume, "RESUME.DOC." Do you realize what a self centered dickhead that makes you? It is grounds for disqualification. How many resumes can someone process if they are all labeled "myresume.doc"? Use your name and date in the file name: "NickSpill resume 20XX.doc" - it's self explanatory and easier to find later. Format the resume in a Word document and a pdf file. A pdf file cannot be so easily manipulated although it might not be readable on some platforms and smart phones.

You might not get a position with a resume, especially when you first start with no training or experience, but you need to furnish one. I know, we have all gotten jobs where submitting a resume was never considered. But, it is better to have one than not have one. Just like your pen, notepad and flashlight. (More on equipment later).

Breaking in - He who hesitates is lost

Back to phone calls because we use our cell phones more than any other tool. There can be no hesitation in your voice. I hear it all the time in phone calls: a hint of uncertainty, a feeling of unease, a lack of confidence. How the hell am I going to hire someone like that? When the shit hits the fan you cannot hesitate, you have to move quickly and decisively. I want decisiveness not arrogance. Again, hearing arrogance or a tone of voice that is too aggressive, too pushy, can be a turn off. If you are like that on the phone, what are you like in person?

Here's an example. My first day on the job with what I soon realized was a difficult family.

We are at a fairground and two of us are looking after a spoiled young man, our dear little overweight Protectee, who has taken over the hoop game. As he has done for the past week, I find out later. The hoop game is in a small amphitheater like setting, very public with crowds walking by. Our little Protectee has all the basketballs that the entire hoop business has and he looks like he will be there for hours. We cannot interrupt him. He has paid in advance, well in advance. Other people, mainly fathers and their sons start to form a line to play the hoop game.

If we tell our little Protectee to hurry up and move on, his father would fire us. So rather than hesitate and wait for an angry line of mothers and fathers to form, we diffuse the situation right away by talking to the parents waiting in line with their children. We do not offer money or other incentives, nor do we lie about the fact that we will only be a few minutes, but we do talk to them and the parents' attention is taken away from the long wait and onto us. We have deflected their hostility. We have to discreetly answer questions, not giving anything away, but we are telling them enough to stop them from complaining and we are giving them something to tell their friends later. "You'd never guess who we were talking to at the park, these two bodyguards, they were telling us all these stories, you wouldn't believe it!"

The stories were made up or exaggerated (and did not involve our present Protectee) but you get the point, we distracted them from their original agenda and got them thinking about something else and we prevented our Protectee and his family from any embarrassment. Later the father complained that we were talking too much to other people and not paying enough attention to his son. He did not understand what we had done. But it did not matter. We stopped anything bad happening and that is always hard to prove. Which brings me to my next point. If you make it look too easy and deflect any hostility or avert an embarrassing moments or avoid a real security situation, the Protectee thinks you are not doing anything.

Nothing bad happened so why did we need you?

I might as well deal with that complaint now because when you are dealing with people who do not understand security and what we do, there is always someone who comes up with this cost saving argument.

"Well, that was a waste of money. Why did we need bodyguards? Nothing happened!"

Nothing happened precisely because we were there and doing our job.

We were there. Our mere presence prevented anything unpleasant from happening. We identified anything that could go wrong and took care of it before it became an issue. You, the Protectee did not even know it happened. Sometimes this is hard to quantify, especially in a close protection team. We are in the protection business. We make sure nothing bad happens. When nothing bad happens, I mean nothing happens, how do we justify our existence?

Every bodyguard who has been in the business for a few years has stories like this: I was part of a protection detail at a bank. Four young men wearing skull caps came in, another came in separately with a large shoulder bag but with a difference, he wore it in the front just like the scene from the opening of the film SNATCH where Benicio Del Toro robs a diamond merchant dressed as a Chasid. The bag looked heavy.

The five young men wore loose fitting clothes, no designer labels, no sports jerseys. Did they have bulletproof vests underneath their bland brandless jerseys? It all looked wrong. These kids would take care to wear fashionable clothing, like sportswear from their basketball idol. They were not there to open an account or cash a check. They had nothing in their hands. The look on their faces when they finally spotted me standing in their way, blocking access to the bank tellers was one of shock. They did not expect to see someone like me. I was there, ready for violence, and they sensed that. I was relaxed and smiling. I knew what they were about to do and was confident I could stop them. They looked at my suit jacket, probably worked out I was wearing a bulletproof vest under my white shirt and tie and that I had a large handgun somewhere on my strong side under my jacket. Then I whispered loud enough into my radio piece in my shirt cuff for their leader to see and hear me.

"All Teams standby! Standby! Standby! Possible bogeys! Repeat bogeys!"

You must think I was being corny or melodramatic but despite the World War Two airman call about bogeys, the message got across loud and clear.

The leader looked at his accomplices, as if to silently question them. They were not expecting such a setup. The look on their faces was priceless. Then they turned to the back entrance, their getaway and saw my partner. Now my partner was freaking out because he had not been paying attention to what had been happening and when he heard that radio call he went into condition red and had his hands in front of him, ready to rip open his black fanny pack where he kept his Beretta, that he had carried since his Special Forces days. His eyes were bug eyed wide!

Meanwhile our little visitors did not know how many of us there were. That was the idea. We were only two but no one was supposed to know that. The bad guys watch B Movies where bank robberies go wrong and they probably thought there was a whole van load of black clad SWAT outside, ready to storm in with heavy artillery.

The four young men looked at each other without saying a word. This was the really interesting part, as it proved to me they had done this before and were fairly confident about working together. They just looked at each other to know what the others were thinking, like a team of predators working together with previous experience. They tried to casually walk out of the bank as quickly as they could. The one with the large bag over his front walked out a little after, also trying to look casual. If you have seen enough criminals about to or considering doing something violent and illegal, it is always a treat to see them retreat with a feigned casualness that just does not look real. None of them were there to cash a check or open an account. They were there to rob the bank. They were there for an armed takeover.

My partner was still frozen by the back door, his hand just about to reach for his Beretta. Once the five were outside he took a deep breath then ran out and got the plate number.

And here is the funny part. At least it is funny now. Not one person in the bank, not even the bank manager and her assistant noticed anything. For the record, they were paranoid about being robbed, as in a real take over bank robbery with multiple robbers and guns. Hence our presence. We had to show them the video play back later after the bank was closed. We did not want to alarm the other bank workers and tellers who had already been robbed a few weeks before hand. At least we got to prove what we did with video documentation. Other times it is more subtle. Who wants to knock over a hard target, a bank that has an unknown number of bodyguards who are watching you and have the jump on you before you decide to rob the bank?

And yes, the Lexus SUV they drove was stolen. We got the plate and with the video stills of their faces we were able to provide the local police with some information. That local police department was not interested in collecting intelligence on possible bank robbers. No crime committed, nothing for them to investigate. That is another bug of mine. We should collect intelligence, information about threats, people, locations, incidents, local stories related to your client or the protection business. The more we know, the better we can protect. Intelligence collection is a vital part of our job. We need to know.

The important part of this operation was that we had prevented something terrible from happening and could document this later. We were lucky. A few seconds later we could have been behind the action versus reaction curve and would not have prevented nor could we have stopped an armed take over of the bank. In cases like this, it is always only a matter of seconds. More on this later, what is called the OODA cycle; Observe, Orient, Decide, Act.

There is a saying that luck is nothing but lots of hard work and preparation. We were in the right place at the right time and had a plan to prevent such a takeover. A few more seconds and five armed bandits would have taken over the bank and two good guys with guns would not have been able to stop them.

Drawing our guns during an armed takeover when four or five men had their handguns out would have been catastrophic for the innocent people in the bank. We would only have endangered the very lives we were there to protect. Who cares about the money? It is insured and the Government can print more. Lives are what we protect.

In times of economic hardship, accountants and other bean counters like to eliminate or reduce security for their company. It looks good in the budget and they reason: "Nothing has happened, so we do not need them."

Or, "Bodyguards for our top executives are too expensive. We have never had an incident so we can eliminate these positions." Or, "Our Clinic has never been attacked. Our doctors know how to look after themselves. We do not need additional security." Or my favorite: "We have the police on speed dial. We don't need armed security in front of our temple." Or the tragically true: "We have a state of the art access control system. No one can get in without a card. We don't need armed security. Besides, we don't like guns."

The above examples are not made up. They were stated in one form or another by committees, boards and organizations that thought they knew about security and cost effectiveness. People died after these decisions were made.

There are many variations for such flawed thinking about security and how much is it worth to protect a life. These are tragic stories fueled by ignorance, prejudice and poor decision-making. For who knows, what will happen in the immediate future. How can you predict imminent threats?

The same flawed thinking applies to budget directors of high-risk entities, abortion clinics, churches, schools, Temples, (Jewish Houses of Worship) and other locations that have been targeted by unpredictable and lone gunmen. Do a news search and see what has happened in these attacks. Unguarded, soft targets have been attacked and people have died. But nothing had happened before so the people responsible for security were saving money by not having effective layered security that included where appropriate, armed and trained security.

A long and detailed argument can be applied across the wide spectrum of protection alternatives from armed security guards to highly trained bodyguards, but I am making a point here. We, as bodyguards, prevent tragedy from happening. That nothing bad happened is our measure of success, not that we shot the attacker at the last moment. The attacker never attacked because we made the target look too hard. We prevented the attack.

Making it look too easy

When I work with my favorite bodyguards, we make everything look so easy. And when we have to work with guys who are not on our level, everything is so much harder! We have it all prepared, advanced, taken care of. Everything flows. The Protectee goes about his business and its as if we are not there but we are. No worries, effortless grace. Now a Protectee who has had a lot of experience with bodyguards will appreciate what we did. (Usually because he has endured a few bad ones, who, thank god, make us look good!)

Successful security guard companies that employ well-trained security guards also make handling security look easy. They can tackle this challenge with technology and customer service. By adapting prescribed radio codes and reporting systems to document all encounters their guards have had with the public, the security companies are able to provide detailed reports with their invoices. So a ten-guard contract might have a thick print out with coded encounters documenting all verbal and other communications that security guards have had with the public. With plain-clothes bodyguards, the process is subtler and it could be just our mere presence or quick verbal communication that averts a situation going from sour to worse. You rarely get to rely on video playback to say: there, we stopped something really bad from happening. Bodyguard agencies though also need to have sound reporting mechanisms to relay to their clients and Protectees what exactly they have done.

Tactical Civility or Verbal Judo by any other term

I've used this technique a lot. Call it verbal judo, tactical civility or just plain common sense communication.

In a penthouse suite, at a private party, I am blocking access to the one toilet everyone can use. My Protectee is in that toilet and doesn't want anyone else in there. An urgent and angry line of drunken people forms. And they all want to know why they cannot go into the bathroom. You know how it is, even adults leave things to the last minute and they are desperate to pee. And god knows what my Protectee is doing in the bathroom. Why is she taking so long? You need to talk to the people waiting. Diffuse any conflict and get them on your side or at least get them into a non-hostile frame of mind, even if they are too drunk to stand and desperately need that bathroom. Having the skill to talk your way into and out of situations helps, a lot. If they start sympathizing with me and how difficult my job is, well, that's a winner. Note, I am not glaring at them and pretending to be a big badass bodyguard. I am communicating with them, even if I am distracting them.

"Two minutes, Turkish!"

"But you said two minutes, five minutes ago!" The English action star replied.

His powerful physique was bursting out of his shirt, he was a little unsteady on his feet, but he laughed at my cockney accent and imitation of his movie lines. Meanwhile the person I was protecting was doing god-knows-what in the bathroom. At least it was her party, and her rooftop hotel suite. The English action star sympathized with me and forgot he desperately needed to go. The rest waited respectfully behind him.

These verbal skills are ultimately more important than knowing how to shoot. You shoot your mouth off every day in some manner, but how often have you shot your gun in public? You will see this material again.

Knowledge not gossip

When planning this book, I did not want to name names, or reveal intimate secrets of celebrities or spread gossip.

To follow the Way, you need knowledge not gossip. So I have excluded naming clients or Protectees. It is the law in Florida anyway. But you do meet down to earth, funny and well-behaved famous people, even in stressful circumstances, and not just waiting in line to go to the bathroom you are guarding.

Back to Bodyguard Schools

There are many questions to ask when interviewing bodyguard schools, and yes, you are going to interview a lot of people regarding the bodyguard school you are planning to attend. This is part of your due diligence, part of your training as a bodyguard. You are not going to plop down a large sum of hard earned money without doing a lot of research are you?

One question to ask is how much time do they spend in role playing, verbal exercises, tactical communications, public encounters that require verbal skills, versus time spent shooting. Yes, it is more fun shooting. How many times are you going to shoot your way out of a complicated escape and evacuation of your Protectee in a crowded urban situation? Probably never. How many times are you going to have to talk your way out of a situation that could quickly escalate from something ugly to something violent? Probably quite a few times, and if you are looking after a particular group of obnoxious Protectees, maybe a lot! So you have to be able to talk your way into and out of situations and your improved tactical civility skills can be very very helpful.

Here we go again about how important it is to be able to talk to people, perfect or imperfect strangers, when you have to. Glaring at someone or pushing them out of the way only works in movies. Although we can all admit, under torture, that it is fun to pick someone up and throw them over a velvet rope or up against a wall when no one is looking or the music is too loud and the lights too low. But who would want to admit to such unprofessional behavior at 4 AM after an endless, endless night?

Knowing when to keep your mouth shut can be a different matter.

I would wager in your career that you will shoot your mouth off rather more than shoot your gun. Am I making my point? Because this is not an original thought. You will find this material in the book: Verbal Judo. You will see this material again and again.

Breaking into the business can come in many different ways: graduating from a top bodyguard school, knowing an agency who will hire you for your first job, being in the right place when someone is hiring a team and you happen to be there with maybe just one reference or your school graduation certificate. You see how this can work? To be in the first profession, you need every contact and skill you have, including social networking with bodyguards, agencies and related businesses. Timing is everything. Whether it is getting pregnant or your first bodyguard detail, you have to be at the right place at the right time doing the right thing.

Chapter Two

The First Profession

Our profession is unique in many ways. We have been called the Fifth Profession. (For an explanation of that you will have to read David Morrell's best selling novel: The Fifth Profession. See the reading guide). But we are more akin to the first profession: we sell our bodies, we get screwed all the time and at the end of the day we can feel all sticky with a bad taste in our mouths. Do you get my point? So what is with the name bodyguard and why do so many in our profession dislike the term?

Look in Genesis and you will find the Hebrew equivalent of bodyguard mentioned where Abraham and Sarah are accompanied with bodyguards. There are bodyguards mentioned throughout the Old Testament. Every King or leader had bodyguards.

The Bible calls them bodyguards, or simply guards. In Hebrew the word reads, in English, SHMR or fill in the vowels, shomer. Shomer means "guard" as in Shomer Rosh, head guard or Hashomer for "the guard" a precursor to the Haganah, but that is another story. Shomer Shabbat means to observe and watch over the Sabbath, the holiest day for observant Jews. Shomer also means to observe or watch over. The Hashomer were also known as watchmen. To observe and guard, ties in with the role of the bodyguard and surveillance and counter surveillance. We watch over our Protectees, we guard, we observe, we protect.

In Samuel 28:2

David said, "*Then you will see for yourself what your servant can do.*" Achish replied, "*Very well, I will make you my bodyguard for life.*"

In Biblical times, bodyguards were servants. It was a lifetime position or until you were killed.

What is in a name?

Bodyguard versus Executive Protection Officer, Close Protection Specialist, VIP Protection Operator

You can call yourself whatever you like. I am down to earth and do not mess around with fancy titles. But some clients like them, hence they have a certain marketing power and as in any business, if it works, use it.

Look in the Old Testament. Who had the first executive protection specialist? What you can't find the VIP close protection officer involved in the contest King Darius proposes to three of his bodyguards, the winner of which gets to rebuild the Temple in Jerusalem? King Darius has guards, bodyguards if you get fancy with the titles. There were no VIP protection specialists back then.

Later in England, King James I and Henry VIII slept with, or next to, or in the same room as their bodyguards. It was common practice to keep your bodyguards close by, real close, even in the dead of night. Not for anything kinky, but for protection and to guard against kidnapping and violent attempts on their regal lives.

I have been on many details where Princes and Princesses always have someone in their bedroom sleeping nearby or with them. No one of royal birth is left unprotected, or alone, not for one minute.

What is the difference between a certified protection specialist, an executive protection agent and a plain old bodyguard? Protection specialist sounds cool and for many in the profession it implies a certain class, better training and a higher level of professionalism. I agree there are many terms better than the plain vanilla term bodyguard. There is no argument that the term bodyguard brings up images of steroid induced thugs, unthinking behemoths and other black suited ruffians with shaven heads and manners to match, but for this book I am using the generic 10 cent word "bodyguard," period.

Many bodyguard schools and associations have elaborate names and labels. You might be able to charge more as a professional protection security officer or an executive protection agent or a close protection officer or a security consultant, the list goes on and on.

A sincere effort has been made to upgrade our profession with descriptive and more professional titles. The general public and the media still refer to us as bodyguards. Look up the word bodyguard in any search engine. All media refer to us as bodyguards as do other writers. (Including the writers in the Bible - yes I know, it's all translated from Aramaic, Hebrew or Greek). Now do a search for the fancy terms such as personal protection specialist and so on. You will only get web sites promoting protection agencies and bodyguard schools.

Whatever your title, your task, your mission, your job is the same: to serve and protect your client or Protectee, at whatever cost, including your life.

In case you are still confused, here is a simple chart outlining the differences.

You can call me what you like, as long as I get paid.

Bodyguard	Protection Specialist
old fashioned name	new professional name
popular meaning	defines better selection
Kevin Costner filmed it	Kevin Costner would never make it
will work for less	more expensive
brawn not brains	brains not brawn
samurai were bodyguards	wear suits not kimonos
fifth oldest profession	graduate of a Protection School

So you still want to be a bodyguard?

Why not be a Law Enforcement officer first?

Consider the difference between the roles of a Law Enforcement officer (LEO) and a bodyguard. One huge difference is steady work and a pension. Unless you are in-house protection for a corporation and have a pension plan, you do not have the job security like a LEO has. If you are 35 and want to get into this business, think ahead 20 years. How much money do you expect to earn? You will experience lots of days with no work, sometimes months off, or you will be faced with the choice of doing low pay security work, just to pay the bills.

If you are considering being a LEO, think of your steady salary, and after 15 to 20 years your fully vested pension. At 55, whom do you think is better off? The LEO or the bodyguard? You do not have to be a math wizard to realize who will earn more in the long run. Things change, your situation is different, and who thinks 20 years ahead when you are young and foolhardy? Yes, there are a handful of bodyguards who are earning more than high-ranking LEOs. But they are just that, a handful, in a very unpredictable and ruthless business where you will always find someone to do your job cheaper and maybe a little better.

Having completed the required years to draw your pension, you can still have a second career as a highly esteemed bodyguard and draw from police experience and contacts as well as that retired badge and ID that counts to many people, especially clients, as validation of your expertise.

Difference between a Law Enforcement Officer (LEO) and a Bodyguard

A bodyguard is fundamentally different from being a local Law Enforcement officer or a Federal agent, apart from the Secret Service and specialized Protection units in various Agencies such as the Diplomatic Protection Service in the State Department or in the U.S. Marshals.

Look at the difference between Law Enforcement and Bodyguards.

Law Enforcement Officer	Bodyguard or VIP Protection Specialist
officer comes home after shift, safe	Protectee comes home, safe
office safety first	Protectee safety first
arrest powers	no arrest powers
reaction	prevention
response to 911 call	pre planning so no 911 call
only on site when called	on site when hired
after action reports	advance planning
trained for investigation and arrest	trained for prevention and protection

Officer Safety versus Protectee Safety

A Law Enforcement officer (LEO) goes home after his or her shift. He has been taught that officer safety comes first. Officer safety is drummed into them at the Academy. For a bodyguard, the Protectee comes home. If you have to give up your life to save your Protectee, then that is part of your job description. We use all masculine examples here but you know we include men and women here equally. Bodyguard safety is only good for protecting the Protectee and getting him out of harm's way. He can always hire another bodyguard. You are expendable. It is not about you.

It is never about you. This fundamental fact escapes a lot of bodyguards who moan and whine about not getting respect or getting assigned horrible jobs or whatever the gripe of the day is. The list can be long, very long. It is always about the Protectee. You do not matter. Period. There is always someone else who can do the job for less and not complain about it. You still want to stand in that corridor? You still want to be a bodyguard?

No Arrest Powers

LEOs have arrest powers. Bodyguards cannot arrest anyone. They have no police powers and can be held to a higher standard than ordinary civilians in that they should be highly trained and knowledgeable about all applicable laws. There are some States where bodyguards have some limited arrest powers but lets not be picky. If you want to wear a badge and carry handcuffs, be a LEO. If Protectee safety comes first, and someone bothers the Protectee are you going to arrest that person? Who is going to look after the Protectee while you make a citizen's arrest? Do you think your Protectee wants to wait around and be further threatened or embarrassed while you make a fool of yourself and the real police arrive?

Just after I wrote this a friend called me. We used to protect the same celebrity and worked well together for years. He told me a new bodyguard was hired by the celebrity we used to work for. The new bodyguard saw a purse-snatcher run down the street towards him and his client. The bodyguard tackled the purse-snatcher and handed him over to the police. The bodyguard was pleased with himself and thought his new Protectee would be proud of him too. The Protectee was livid. "What are you doing? Who cares about a purse-snatcher? Your job is to look after me." The Protectee had to wait around as more police arrived and questioned all the witnesses and his hero bodyguard. The bodyguard had created an insecure environment for the Protectee as people swarmed around him wanting autographs and cell phone photos and videos. The rapidly growing crowd was immediately texting, tweeting and Facebooking their friends. The Protectee was very annoyed. He was trapped in a very public situation. He is always polite to fans and always accommodates them for photos and autographs. The bodyguard was fired.

Reaction versus Protection

LEOs react to situations, they respond to emergency calls. Bodyguards prevent bad situations from happening. An officer in a patrol car is multitasking, responding to many incidents, taking prioritized calls from the dispatcher and he is under direct supervision of his Sergeant. A bodyguard has one task, protect a particular Protectee. With proper planning by the bodyguard there is no need to call for emergency help. A bodyguard can also be on a dedicated site, a particular location next to the Protectee. A LEO is protecting a community, on patrol and has to respond to a location, a specific call. They have a wide geographical area to look after, a lot of people to protect and serve. Bodyguards are close to their Protectee.

A phone call away versus a footstep away

How many times have I heard:

"Don't worry lady, we're only a phone call away." And,

"We'll drive by your house several times on our shift. You're in safe hands."

Such a strategy does not make for around the clock on site protection. You have heard the horror stories concerning domestic violence. A woman is threatened. She acquires a restraining order, a court order forbidding the threat, the man, usually, from being within a certain distance from her. A piece of paper does not stop a determined stalker or attacker. In some cases it can inflame the already unstable person.

The woman sees the attacker and calls the police. They tell her to lock her doors and windows. By the time any help arrives, it is too late. The attacker has already committed the act of violence and disappeared before the police arrive.

A hired bodyguard on site to protect would deter if not stop a potential attack. We all have stories about sitting in a car all night in a driveway waiting for the angry ex-husband or boyfriend to show up. He does, but he sees the car in the driveway, a man looking at him from inside the car, maybe getting out of the car to meet and greet the ex. But the ex drives away, unwilling to confront an armed bodyguard hired by his former wife. We have prevented a confrontation, at least for that night. More on this later as it is not enough just to stop an expected attack happening for one night. Sometimes having a car with a bodyguard inside at night might not be the correct short-term protective solution. The solution has, of course, to be more permanent, and we are not talking "movie permanent" like shooting the ex, but rather a successful and peaceful resolution to the conflict. Of course another "peaceful solution" is prison time for the person doing the threatening.

Crime Reports versus Advance Planning

LEOs write after action reports, arrest and incident reports. A bodyguard writes up advance plans so there is no need for an incident to happen or an after action report. The threat has been foreseen, anticipated and dealt with or prevented. Prevention and protection belongs to the bodyguard. Investigation, after the bad event had happened, and arrest, belongs to the LEO.

Maturity is earned, one day, one year at a time

If you are familiar with elite bodyguard teams you will see a fair number in their 40's and older, in great shape and looking sharp. They have completed their military or police service and are drawing pensions and they are working. They have the experience and are pulling two checks, one from their pension, one from their new profession. What could be better?

I always advise younger ambitious men and women who want to get into the protection business to get military then Law Enforcement experience before moving into the bodyguard world. If they cannot deal with close supervision and authority, how will they work in a structured environment with other bodyguards, team leaders and the Protectee? Nothing beats learning from direct experience, extensive training and exposure to diverse stressful episodes. You cannot learn this from reading a book. Which leads me to the next topic, bodyguard schools.

Chapter Three

The Bodyguard School Solution and the Importance of Training

To work as a bodyguard in the United States you will have to be licensed in your State. Some States have no licensing. Others make it rather difficult. There are sites on the web that will tell you exactly what you have to do in each State. Google the words "bodyguard licensing" - and your "State," other keywords are "private investigator" and "security guard." In the U. K., there is an elaborate licensing and accreditation bodyguard and security personnel program, quite an evolution from just licensing doormen. In the U. K. to work in close protection you need to be licensed by the Security Industry Authority (S.I.A.).

The best way to break into the business, with the correct licensing of course, is through a reputable Bodyguard School. There are several top rated schools in the U.S. There is no guarantee that once you graduate from a school, or two, that you will ever find a suitable job. And once you do win that first job, then your on-the-job training really begins. Say goodbye to fixed shifts, dependable hours, guaranteed bathroom breaks, time to eat regular meals, you get the idea, your life as you know it, is over, you are working for someone else, and your priorities and work breaks are of no consequence. I am exaggerating but only for some jobs.

There are also some great bodyguard schools in other countries, but unless you are working in that country I would advise against the extra expense of traveling there and paying their tuition. Why? Three words, networking, networking,

networking. You need to be able to network with people in your own country. You want to work after you have graduated, right? There is always an exception and here it would be Israel. They have their own security methods and protection principles honed by over 60 years of being at war. Being Israeli-trained carries some cache in some knowledgeable circles. Again cost is a factor.

If you are leaving the Military or Law Enforcement or want to upgrade from being a bouncer or security guard, enroll in a premier Bodyguard School. The School will probably not like the term bodyguard. Remember the chart in the previous chapter: the difference between Law Enforcement and Bodyguards. No offence but bodyguards and cops live in different worlds.

Some of the best schools can be found by typing in "Bodyguard School" in the search engine of your choice. Do your own research, find one that suits you, your budget and book the course. We have excellent bodyguard schools that offer proper training and allow you the opportunity to network and develop contacts for future jobs. You have to do your own research and find the best fit for yourself. You have to do your own advance.

What is this term Advance?

It's used as a verb and a noun. We advance our itinerary, our travel plans. That means we research, rehearse and plan for every contingency for a prescribed schedule. A valuable and mundane example is advancing a vacation with the wife.

I arrange and book everything I can in advance. Hotels, travel from the airport, rental cars, other transportation, and so on. I look at maps; use Google Earth and other satellite photos to get an idea of any unknown terrain, if I am unfamiliar with the territory. I plan for every contingency. I have lists and schedules for the theater, films, festivals, restaurants, museums and other places of attractions we might be interested in. I have identified emergency dentists and doctors as well as hospital contact information. I have a prepared folder containing every piece of information I might need, to make my vacation a worry free, smooth series of fun and relaxing events.

Or as they say in the military: "Proper Prior Planning Prevents Piss Poor Performance."

The wife sees the big black folder, thinks I am anal retentive, but I have everything I need, even if she wants to go to a different restaurant or change the schedule, I have easy access to that information. I did my advance properly. Of course this can all be stored and accessed from a smart phone now, but it pays to have paper backup.

Advance your own bodyguard school

The same prior planning is needed when executing your due diligence in selecting your bodyguard school. Such self-directed research further helps to qualify you as a bodyguard. While conducting "protection missions," you will have opportunities to advance certain situations, check out a certain place, a particular location. To advance a location is central to being a good bodyguard, knowing what is going to happen, when and where. For instance, you are taking your Protectee to a restaurant. You have time to go there beforehand, meet the Maitre D, wait staff, select a suitable table or tables, brief everyone on how to act (if necessary) and work out entrances and exits, check the toilets, kitchen and so on. You also know where to pull up in the car or vehicles and how to make a quick get away and where the emergency exits are and alternative escape and evasion points as well as any traffic and parking issues.

Selecting a bodyguard school is like conducting an advance for your security detail. You check out the school as much as you can, interview recent graduates, talk to staff, read up on internet posts, web sites, and do as much information collection as you can. If you post an inquiry on an e-group, or discussion group or forum related to bodyguards and security, do not write something inane like: "Which is the best bodyguard school?" That is like posting "What is better, Microsoft or Apple?" back in 1991. That shows how uninformed you are. Try and be more specific. Identify certain schools you have thoroughly researched and ask specific questions about them. Then ask for comments from people who have attended that school, off line. That is, do not post such communications for everyone to read. You want to enter into an e-mail dialogue with a graduate of that school and find out the good and the bad, without that graduate having to defend his choice or reputation to a bunch of lurking know-it-alls. Try and think of innovative ways to elicit truthful and perceptive responses from people who have actually graduated from these schools rather than e-group commandos who have many opinions but little experience and too much time to post worthless comments on the bulletin boards. The Golden rule on these types of e-groups and boards is: if you are posting too much, you are not working and if you are not working, you ain't that good!

It's your advance, your money and your graduation certificate.

Then you ask yourself some tough questions.

Wouldn't you rather be working and earning money rather than spending money on training, especially when there are no guarantees that you will be hired because of your elite bodyguard school graduate status?

If you are already working as a bodyguard why go to school and interrupt your income?

Can you learn just as much with on the job training with experienced bodyguards acting as mentors?

If you have no time to train, why bother? If you are working all the time you must be good? Right?

For every argument there is a counter argument.

I know bodyguards who never went to a top rated elite bodyguard school and they are very good at their job. They learned the hard way, with on the job training and following the lead bodyguard. And they thought for themselves, as in how can I do this better, smarter, safer and perhaps cheaper, for we are running a business.

I have worked with some awesome bodyguards who have graduated from top rated bodyguard schools. Then I have worked with guys whom I have wondered, how did they graduate? What does anyone see in them? I would not hire them. Why is someone else hiring them?

You are going to get this all the time in the highly opinionated, highly testosterone charged and highly argumentative and at times, contentious bodyguard business. But it is not the Way of the Bodyguard. There are plenty of insecure, jealous, and ignorant men out there posing as bodyguards and experts in personal protection and all manner of deadly arts. Everybody is an expert.

What training do you need to be a bodyguard?

Every skill is perishable

Back to the positive. Training is positive. Every skill you have is perishable. Without adequate practice and training, how can you become better, let alone maintain your current skills?

What skills do you need and what training will help you in improving these skills?

Interestingly, it's the basics that Schools cover that you need, such as how to walk, how to talk and how to act in certain situations. It's a particular mindset, how to protect, how to react to certain situations and how to take care of the Protectee if something unusual happens. I stated this is not a bodyguard training text; there are several very comprehensive manuals in print plus specially produced ones you will get at your chosen bodyguard school.

What I am interested in is how you think, how you will take the path towards becoming an excellent bodyguard. I have called this, the Way of the Bodyguard, as it is a process, a journey, a series of discoveries about who you are and what you can become. That is why training is so important. Training is endless.

The same principle of maintenance and improvement applies to your body as it apples to your mind. Even if you are working long hours and do not get enough sleep, you still need to perform some kind of physical training regime to keep your level of fitness.

Why all the emphasis on physical training?

To find your Way as a bodyguard you have to find your balance between training and working. Bear in mind that your skills are perishable, but you should not be.

You can never get enough training. No matter what you do, if you are not training to get better, you are getting worse. As Lt. Col. Dave Grossman (The Bulletproof Mind - see required reading) says: "When the shit hits the fan, you do not rise to the occasion, you sink to the level of your training." You will see this again.

I want to illustrate this principle that you sink to the level of your training with a gruesome story.

What happens if you only fire your gun once a year for your re-qualification at the range and your only firearms training is watching John Wayne movies? Then you are caught in a gang hold up and you forget the first rule in an armed confrontation: action is faster than reaction.

I came across this unfortunate security guard at the local morgue. There is no dignity and immense sadness seeing an older man, terribly out of shape, lying naked on a stainless steel table. His dead body told a tragic story.

I had heard about the shooting two days before, when I had one of my bodyguards looking after another client. This client's brother was the Lieutenant in the Rescue truck that responded to the security guard shooting. The client told me from his brother's perspective the aftermath to the shooting. It only reinforced to my client how dangerous Miami was and that he was wise to have protection for his business down here.

I was at the morgue looking after another client. Now that is a long story. And not for publication ever. Suffice to say I looked after this person from coma to ashes and made sure there was never any photo taken of him. I accomplished that mission but while attending that autopsy, the Medical Examiner pulled me over and gave me a lecture on the security guard, the other corpse laid out.

I already knew the guard had been inside the jewelry store. A gang of young men, who had based themselves on another older and more ruthless crew, the so-called Rolex Gang, had cased the store and then rushed inside wearing masks and brandishing handguns.

The guard saw a young man in a mask run up to him with a 9mm pistol pointed at him. What is the first lesson in a situation like this? You can learn this painfully in Simunition or paint ball training: action is faster than reaction. You cannot out draw someone who already has a gun pointed at you and his finger is on the trigger. It only happens in John Wayne movies, not in real life.

The robber saw the guard try to pull out his revolver from his holster as he got off the chair. What was the guard thinking in the last moments of his life? He could have just raised his hands and said, "Please don't hurt anyone. Take what you want. We're cool."

The robber had no choice but to fire at the attacking security guard. From his perspective it was self defense, self-preservation. The robber or the guard. And the robber had a huge advantage. He was approaching the guard with his finger on the trigger. It was easy to squeeze that trigger, he did not have to think, the security guard was trying to get his gun out of his holster to shoot the robber. The robber was already hyped up, his heart rate was pounding at a higher rate, he automatically aimed and fired, to protect himself from being shot. The robber was committed to squeeze the trigger at such short range. The guard never gave him a choice. Would the guard have been saved had he put his hands up? We will never know. He never gave the robber that opportunity. Now that is something we stress in Simunition training when we recreate scenarios like this. If you back down, surrender to a robber, you might just save your life and those around you. Of course this does not work for suicide bombers or robbers intent on suicide by cop or security guard, or someone unhinged on drugs or having a mental breakdown, so you cannot second guess.

The one 9mm bullet fired from the semi automatic was a full metal jacket, not a soft nose or jacketed hollow point.

The medical examiner showed me the path of the bullet. It went though his chest; the shock wave blew out his aorta. It then continued to travel through his body, through his spine and out of his back. The guard collapsed and was dead before he hit the floor. The bullet kept traveling until it was stopped by the wall opposite the guard. Crime scene personnel dug the bullet out of the wall. It still had traces of blood and bone of the guard on it.

Rescue tried shocking him then massaging his heart. He was airlifted to Trauma One in minutes and the trauma team cut him open, gave him massive blood transfusions and massaged his heart. I saw the emergency incisions they had made in his chest. It was chilling and humbling at the same time to see how much work and care the Trauma One personnel had applied to the security guard. All the work they had put into trying to save him, to bring him back from the dead. All to no avail. He was dead on arrival. He was dead, the Medical Examiner told me again, before he hit the floor of the store.

I felt privileged to see what had happened to him and to have seen the cadaver on the table. That the trauma personnel had tried to bring him back from the dead was awe-inspiring.

Here was a brutal and horrific lesson that everyone in this business must come to terms with. Faced with a no win situation and perhaps being caught off guard, a little negligent, not paying attention when you should have been, you still need to know how to act. You will only know how to act if you have been trained. When the shit hits the fan you sink to the level of your training. You do not rise to the occasion. And on occasions like that, a bulletproof vest helps and could save your life.

This commentary is in no way a criticism of the guard and his actions. I do not want to disparage his memory or his heroic act of confronting an armed robber who had a gun pointed at him. I was honored to stand next to his cadaver and witness what had happened to him. I can in no way second guess his responses and what actually happened to him. I am merely illustrating some basic concepts regarding certain stressful situations and the fateful outcome. And here is the chilling reality to long shifts in security and bodyguard work; you can never be totally aware all the time, there are moments when you are not paying attention. We have all drifted off into a white zone, a daydream, for seconds, sometimes minutes. It comes with long shifts, standing around, waiting for something bad to happen. We are all guilty of not paying attention 100% of the time. You cannot be totally switched on all the time. Our minds, our attention wanders, if only for a few seconds.

Role Playing and Training

Yes, you can spend a lot of money on amazing tactical shooting courses or enroll in your local paintball club but to really learn how to react to certain situations you have to role play them, work through some basic scenarios and game plan them. What works, what doesn't work and how can you improve your survivability and protect your Protectee?

Now the poor guard was protecting a bunch of watches and stones. His mission was not to protect directly the lives of the people in the store. But, he lost his life and put other people's lives in danger by acting like he did. I am not being a Monday morning quarterback here because I do this training and I have written Manuals about how to act and react in security guard and bodyguard roles and situations.

Some situations are not winnable. You find this out the hard way when you die in training, not through dying in real life.

Lets analyze the guard shooting in a high value jewelry store that is open to the public. There are no double gates or other controlled access devices to the store, just the front doors and windows that clearly give a view of the mall outside.

When you are in a static position as a bodyguard and have to look after and secure a particular space, there is always a specific area where you can dominate the entire space. It is usually close to or near an entrance and with a good vantage point for the rest of the space. Ask five bodyguards where this position is and you might get five different answers but what is important here is that you have worked out this situation and you think you are in the best possible position.

Now back to the guard in the jewelry store.

If you are the security guard you need to be in a position of dominance in that store. You need to be able to see clearly the entrance and the immediate vicinity around the entrance to the store. So you will be almost always near the entrance, moving around so as not to get bored, moving the feet, and sitting down as little as possible. You also do not want someone to come up behind you, so you are mindful of your position in the entire store. I know some bodyguards can stand all day and do not complain. Put them in a guard stance and say stay and they will. Rare individuals I've found. Most men want to move around, sit down, take breaks, chat up the ladies. But we are talking here about a low wage and poorly trained security guard rather than a highly trained and better paid (we hope) bodyguard. There is a difference. But with bad timing and a few minutes, maybe a few seconds of inattention, the tragic result could have been the same.

Like I said, I am not sitting in judgment here. A guard was shot dead, doing his duty. Now I ask you, if you carry a gun for a living, how many times a year do you go to the range to shoot? Do you have a course of fire you set yourself, or goals you aspire to? Or do you just blow a lot of holes in paper targets with no disciplined plan and you wonder why there are holes all over your target? How many training courses do you complete each year? Do you just qualify on the range and that is it? Or do you practice at the range on a more regular basis with specific plans and goals in mind? In Florida, armed security guards and bodyguards have to qualify once a year. Most Law Enforcement agencies also qualify once a year. The FBI qualifies their Special Agents four times a year. What does that tell you? How many times do you qualify a year? How many times do you go to the range?

What about holster practice and dry firing?

Do you practice holster draws wearing your usual equipment and clothes, and an empty gun of course? How often do you practice these holster draws? Do you time yourself? Do you go through various scenarios? Can you clear your house in the dark from one room to the next and backwards? How much game playing do you do, tactically, with your firearm or other arms or flashlights? How often do you dry fire your handgun? What sort of routines do you do when practicing dry firing? Do you practice in low light conditions?

Training is endless.

With any complex physical activity, you are either getting better or getting worse. To train properly, is to improve. To not train and slouch through each day as if it were just like the last, is to regress. If you have attained a level of peak fitness (especially for a certain sport) you know how your body feels under such conditions. It's a feeling you never want to lose. Of course you cannot maintain that level of optimum fitness for a long time but you can be in a state of reliable fitness, a state where you know you can operate for long periods under stress without failing. How do you maintain that level?

Working out and training. There is a difference.

You workout regularly to attain and keep a level of fitness and readiness to do your job: protecting people effectively.

You train at specific skills so that you can improve your job of protecting and serving people effectively.

By that, I mean maintaining a certain level of fitness physically, and also working on and improving certain skills you specifically need.

You can work out every day, executing a workout program that is right for you. Even if its only 15 to 20 minutes. Better to work out for a short intense period in your living room or hotel room every day than put off that two hour killer workout in a gym that is an hour's drive from your home that you never seem to have the time for. When a rather rotund man waddles up to me and I see his belly hanging over his belt and that third chin working its way above his soup stained tie, I am not, nor is the client, impressed. The "waddler" is going to say "I don't have time for working out, I'm always working." Good. Work somewhere else for low pay.

If you look the part, you might just get the part and you cannot look the part unless you do actually project a level of health and fitness and readiness that will inspire confidence in your Protectee.

Your Protectee has to look at you and think, yes that guy looks strong and capable of protecting me. Look at yourself in the mirror. Would you hire yourself to protect you?

Hardly a fair question to an egomaniac or someone without self-awareness. But if you would not hire yourself to protect your own family, your loved ones, who would want to hire you?

The Importance of Continuing Education

Nothing looks more impressive on a resume (there is a big caveat here but you will have to read about that later) than a series of very reputable certifications for specific skills related to bodyguard work from well-known and accredited sources and schools.

So why train?

If you watch old masters in any martial art, no matter what school or discipline they possess, they always work through basic techniques, basic exercises. You can be 70 years old and still do the same exercises you did when you were 17, crunches, pull ups, push ups, freestanding squats, all basic bodyweight high repetition exercises. The same with martial arts moves, blocks, punches, pushes, take downs and sidesteps. Simple basic moves.

While we are talking basics, we need to address "talking," being able to communicate to the right people what you want them to do or say for you. 'Talking" seems too plain, so "Tactical Verbal Communications" sounds better.

Tactical Verbal Communication Skills Training

Do not forget to ask the Bodyguard school what they will do for your verbal communication skills. According to verbal judo doctrine, an uncocked tongue is more dangerous than an uncocked gun. We use our mouth more than we use our guns. You have to do more than just read Verbal Judo. I am quoting George Thompson here. Take a course or two and apply the principles in everyday life. But you still have to read the book. It is required reading. And once you have read it, read it again. I have stopped buying and giving copies away. Now I make new bodyguards buy their own.

What can be more powerful than using your own words to change other people's behavior, to get them to do what you want them to do while protecting your client and not causing any incidents, but making the Protectee's life easier?

What you cannot change - what and who you are

There are certain qualities that you cannot change. These inherent traits are something you have to live with. I know mine, especially as my wife reminds me all the time. I did not say weaknesses, I said traits. As we like to say when working large details and there is a mix of personalities, we all have our strengths.

If you have been a bodyguard long enough, you will have encountered such weaknesses, not from Protectees as much as from other bodyguards.

The term "overly impressed with himself" comes to mind when dealing with certain men in our profession, not to be confused with "bustling with confidence." Sometimes the other bodyguards can be more of a threat than the expected threat itself.

Then there is Post Traumatic Stress Disorder, PTSD. I have employed young men who have just returned from a war zone and they have adapted well to civilian life again. But PTSD can manifest itself in strange and unexpected ways. We have all been through stressful situations, some more stressful than others, as in seeing our mates, our team blown up, or worse, if there is such a thing. Such experiences do not go away. And we can have no control over how PTSD emerges or interacts with our ordinary lives. We all handle it differently. Then there are bodyguards who are too high-strung and see threats everywhere.

We had one particular duo who were looking after a Middle Eastern family in Los Angeles. I had no say over who worked with whom on this detail, so I just had to watch the drama unfold. The duo seemed to attract trouble. Every day they sensed or witnessed a possible attack. One night on Rodeo Drive they leapt out of their chase car and drew their guns on two other Middle Eastern gentlemen whom they had seen in the same hotel and whom they thought had been following their Protectee too closely. We had an off-duty local police officer on our detail who patched things up afterwards.

On the brighter side, bodyguards on opposing teams, can work together.

We were in Las Vegas. We were protecting a high roller who was attending a particularly high profile convention and had just left a large company under disagreeable terms. An associate of mine was protecting the surviving owner of the same company who told his bodyguards that our Protectee had been fired, given a large cash payment but was still a viable threat and could attack him. The situation had escalated as they lived and worked a few miles from each other and were trading law-suits and insults.

The bodyguards got together. We coordinated our sched-ules. We knew where the other team was, so we avoided any confrontation. It was not cheating, it was working together. Sometimes the simplest solution is the best. Both Protectees were very happy and thought they had out witted the other. We all got paid. The lawyers back home worked out an agreement our Protectees could all live with.

So where is the list of approved Bodyguard schools?

It was not disingenuous to omit this list. It was intentional. Why should I give you a list of schools? This is not the Way. This is a learning experience and you have enough skills and ideas presented here to find your own best school to attend, if you feel this is the Way for you. We all have our personal jour-ney and if it includes a Bodyguard school for you that is great, because you will find the right school by extensive research not from calling a phone number printed here.

What are the qualities of a bodyguard to follow the Way?

Chapter Four

Qualities of a Bodyguard

We all have our own individual approach to being a bodyguard. Just looking the part as portrayed in movies does not work. (Check out Chapter Eleven: Bodyguards in Film). Even if you have a massive presence, you still have to be a good communicator, and gifted in verbal judo.

I am standing outside a door with a new bodyguard I've never worked with before. He is the strong silent type, 300 lbs with a shaved head and a black suit. To start the conversation I say, "Nice boots." He replies, "Yeah, I always like to break in new boots with blood. I can't wait to kick someone's teeth in." Oh is this going to be a lovely night. I never worked with him again and he probably thought I was a wuss because I talked several people out of violence that night.

Call it what you want, but being able to talk people into doing or not doing certain acts is critical. Whether you have to interact with a concierge, a doorman, an obnoxious drunk or the Protectee's girlfriend, knowing how to talk to each individual and handle the situation is a skill that needs to be honed.

If you enroll in an expensive bodyguard course make sure they present an intense verbal judo class, there are lots of role-playing situations and that verbal and non-verbal communications are covered in depth. You can do all the firearms courses you can afford but if you cannot use and control your tongue then how dangerous are you to your Protectee?

Essential Qualities

The essential qualities I look for in a bodyguard, are as follows:

ETHICS and INTEGRITY

It's a mixed bag, ethics. Lawyers are taught ethics in Law School now. There is a place to teach ethics to bodyguards as well; what, when and how to do the right thing.

Then there is a higher concept, integrity. You either have it or you don't. There is no in-between. It is like the digital world, it is either a 1 or a 0. There is nothing else. 1 or 0. You either have integrity or you do not.

A NYPD friend of mine told me this story some time ago but its still relevant now for separating those with integrity and those without. It is not just about honesty or having a strong ethical bias.

The story he told went like this: cops get a lesson with the first drug bust they walk into. There is $180,000 on a mattress. The two drug dealers are handcuffed and escorted out of the room. There are three of you in that room. No one else knows about the cash. The drug dealers are going to lie about how much money was on the mattress and no one will believe them anyway. That's $60,000 each or if you leave $90,000, there is still $30,000 each. It is tempting. More cash money than you have ever seen. There are temptations like this all the time. How would you act? And how would you act if the others have already agreed to split the cash and you have to go along, to be accepted by them?

I have worked jobs for another agency where the Protectee or his company have approached me and told me they want to work with me directly. Can they hire me and pay me? I politely tell them that I am under contract with the agency they hired and I cannot accept their offer. I know plenty of bodyguards who would not think about betraying the agency that originally hired them. I know because I have had such bodyguards turn on me and try to steal my clients. This is a cutthroat business where sometimes the scariest characters are other bodyguards, including the ones on your own team.

Integrity is either 1 or 0. You are honest or you are a thief. You either declare all the money or you steal. There is no middle ground, no grey area to debate.

The same goes for integrity with the Way of the Bodyguard. You remain loyal to your team, your agency, your Protectee (within legal limits) and you always do the right thing.

So the first quality I look for in a bodyguard is: does he have integrity?

SELF-AWARENESS

Does he know himself? Is he at peace with who he is?

He can be hungry, have an offbeat sense of humor, but he still has to have that discernable quality I call inner peace. Someone who won't get ruffled when the shit hits the fan. Someone who has nothing to prove, because he has proved himself many times and has no need to put his team and his Protectee in danger to show how tough he is.

Arrogance and self-awareness do not go together. The more mature bodyguards have usually worked this out. That is why you see guys in their 40's and 50's working together. They know the routine, have nothing to prove and just want to get the job done right and go home.

INSTINCTS and OPENNESS

Does he have good instincts? Can you trust his intuition that is enhanced by experience.

Is he more than just streetwise, is he able to sense when things are about to go wrong and take appropriate action? Can he process unusual situations in real time and act and react accordingly?

This is where working with a former street cop can be so beneficial. I've worked with some great NYPD undercovers. Years of successfully completing street operations and surveillances have developed their instinctive reactions and their intuition to a high degree.

There we were in a new city, stuck in a 3 AM traffic jam. I was stuffed into the back of a large rented SUV with nervous impatient rappers. They had just performed at a club and wanted to leave the area quickly. I was at one window, my partner, the former NYPD undercover detective who was now a bodyguard, was scanning the other side of the street.

All the nightclubs in the area had just closed and there were a lot of stoned and drunk people on the streets and in large vehicles, bumper to bumper. There was loud music, people checking each other out from their vehicles. A suspicious young male lurked in the bushes nearby. By the term suspicious, I mean there was no reason for this young man, with baggy clothing and hands we could not see, to hide in the bushes. He was not going to the bathroom and he was not waiting for a rendezvous. He would be a prime candidate for the "what is wrong with this photo?" contest.

I was looking in the other direction. Then my partner had his gun out and whispered a calm precise commentary on what he was seeing. He was very alert, very aware and I was thinking Holy Crap! He saw all this and I was only just processing it. The suspicious young male hiding in the bushes would have seen three guys come out of our vehicle. We had our guns at our sides and scanned the area around him. We did not have tunnel vision, but we were closely watching him. If he had opened fire, he would have received a wall of lead.

He walked slowly backwards until he got to the side of the building, then he ran. Did he have bad intentions? We never gave him an opportunity to find out. We could not have had an escape and evacuation plan with our vehicle, as we were stuck in dense traffic. Our only choice was to present a harder target, one with overwhelming force.

That was just another night dealing with paranoid rappers. Preventing bad things from happening is what we do. We do not get into out of control shootings in a city where we have no influence and where the local police would have been extremely hostile.

We got our group to the airport and they flew off in their G4. Then I heard about the incident that happened previously and why the current incident had such resonance for them. Protectees always seem to leave out the important stuff, like what happened the last time they visited this city and how their best friend was shot coming out of a nightclub. In the same place and same time of night. This information would have been good to know.

There were no holes in my bulletproof vest. No one got arrested. I got paid in $5 bills that smelled of a herb. Memo to self. Do not work for these people again. Despite their own head of security being a dear friend and great bodyguard, they as a group, were a constant risk-magnet. I needed to apply my instincts to client selection as well. This is dealt with later when I write about who is your real client?

My father had incredible instincts. He could sense events before they happened. When I was a kid, he could call a train before it arrived at the station and before I could hear it with my young ears. Years of being shelled by Japanese field artillery in Burma had honed his timing and instincts to where he could sense when something would happen, call it or avoid it. Up until his last years he never had a car accident, or any accident. He always knew when to change or avert his course. His sense of timing was exquisite.

To have good instincts, you need to be open to learning more. This sense of openness is not just a measurable character trait but a real asset when following the Way. How do you get better at your profession? You keep learning, improving your instincts and your skills. How many men have you met who act as if they know everything? Who are superior to you? And who will not learn anything, because they really think that they know it all? Such men are very dangerous and are to be avoided. They also have lousy or non-existent instincts. They substitute previous experience, which can be extensive, for using their untrained instincts.

Openness, a solid working street sense and a highly developed intuition, all work together.

PHYSICAL AND MENTAL CONDITIONING

Is he in good physical condition, not necessarily huge and muscular, but can he survive a long grueling day with no breaks, intense demands and still exhibit grace and calm under pressure?

This entails mental toughness as well. I believe being in good, not necessarily top physical condition, is part of being in sound mental condition as well. One of the most important qualities Special Forces selection committees look for is that mental toughness, not that you are physically a superman, but that you have the mental ability to achieve your mission, no matter the obstacles.

HUMOR

Can he laugh at himself? Does he have a sense of humor?

A highly developed sense of humor is an indication of intelligence. Humor releases stress and develops a perspective on what we do. A humorless bodyguard could be a time bomb waiting to explode. Do you like working with people who have short tempers, always seem to be angry and can never see the absurdity or the humor in their situation? Being able to have that humorous perspective has saved many a tedious and ridiculous job, when you can laugh with a fellow bodyguard and develop an objective view on your current situation.

We were in a parking lot when a tow truck unexpectedly entered our supposedly secure space. The very large bodyguard I was working with pulled out his little revolver. Everything looked little next to him. He was built like a large brick wall and had matching intelligence and no sense of humor. I talked to the tow truck driver who was scanning the parking lot and looking at us. He never got out of his cabin. "I must be in the wrong place!" He uttered and backed out rather quickly.

I turned to my Hulk who said, "I didn't know what to do. I couldn't shoot him. Could I?"

"You did great." I reassured him. "Your presence alone scared him off. You didn't need to draw your weapon. But he got the message."

I made a mental note not to put him in any taxing mental situations again. He might not know what to do if the threat did not retreat from his presence.

For the next hour, I had to listen to a stream of theories about what could have happened to him and the tow truck driver. A little humor would have helped this tedious debriefing.

But he did have a great physical presence and he was marvelous backstage for touring rock groups. He could deal with physical fans who turn fanatic and he knew how to move and protect his Protectees. As we say in the Bodyguard business, we all have our strengths.

PHYSICAL PRESENCE

Does he have a physical presence?

He does not have to be 6 foot 3 inches and 235 pounds of hard muscle with close-cropped hair to look intimidating. It sure helps but a smaller, lighter man can still project a professional and no-nonsense presence. There should be a quality in his eyes and an authority in the way he holds himself that projects a firm measure of intelligent protection. I have worked with many men who are less tall than me but still project a strong presence, without trying. They are not small men trying to be over 6 foot tall, they are just sure of themselves. And in many difficult situations I have looked up to such men.

We were in a new town, and a new hotel. I had flown in Alex as I needed back up. Alex was not a big man but I felt safe when I was working with him. I knew our younger Protectee who liked to go out clubbing was going to create problems. I had worked with Alex for three years before I found out he had been awarded the Navy's Silver Star. He never talked about what he had done. He never talked. The first night Alex was hired, we were in a nightclub with a rather rowdy group of people and our Protectee. A couple of very large thugs tried to move in on the women who were entertaining our party and they obviously wanted to pick a fight with our Protectee. Before I could do anything, Alex was in their faces and he managed, without creating too much noise to get them out of our way and out of the nightclub. Then he returned to take up his position near our party as if nothing had happened. Compared to what I discovered later about him, this little incident was nothing, but goes to prove how effective some bodyguards are regardless of size, weight or hair length. Physical presence means a lot more.

TRAINING

Does he have the desire to keep training?

The Way of the Bodyguard follows the quest for perfection, and endless training is part of that quest. Is he hungry to learn new techniques, new ideas, new ways of doing things? Can he keep on training, improving himself, even after weeks of 12 to 16 hour shifts? Training is endless. I know I am starting to sound repetitive about this one mantra but its true – train or die. Ask anyone coming back from combat in some far away country. What saved their life when things went bad? Training saved them, a lot of training specific to their combat situations.

Common Sense Self Defense

I try to practice what I preach. I was introduced to Grand Master Bram Frank and his teachings years ago. Influenced by Filipino knife fighting, kali, and escrima, Bram also draws on JuJitsu, and real life close quarter combat. His teachings are based on reality, on actual combat, hence he flies around the world teaching elite Commando and Special Forces units, year after year. They love training with him because they use his methods and they work. There is no greater proof of the effectiveness of his teachings in the endorsement of so many warriors.

For bodyguards using less lethal methods, small movements and deflections, make sense when you have to use some kind of physical force. Bram Frank calls this approach Common Sense Self Defense combat. Check your favorite search engine for Bram Frank's YouTube videos and other sites extolling and demonstrating his teachings. His philosophy and easy to learn skills will play an important part in the use of intermediate force in deflecting or de-escalating conflicts around your Protectee.

Among Bram Frank's top instructors whom I have trained with is Shuki Drai, an ex-IDF Special Forces soldier and bodyguard who runs his own school, Mixed Defensive Tactics Street Combat. Shuki brings real life experience and tactical knowledge to dealing with bodies in motion that threaten and need to be contained.

An interesting phenomenon that has evolved over the last few years is a loose network of like minded martial artists and trainers who have informally worked together, shared ideas and training concepts. In your local area, there are probably instructors who also tap into this informal network. I see this network evolving through traveling instructors giving seminars, local instructors attending each other's workshops and links through social network sites. This spirit of sharing and learning and training with each other, across schools and disciplines is a far cry from when I trained under my Sensei in the 1980's. Before the advent of the Mixed Martial Arts approach to fighting and self-defense, different schools and Sensei were very territorial about what they taught and shared.

Now, we are much more open. Egos have been deflated with real world experience and the truth of combat in an enclosed ring. I like to think we are making progress.

Then there is a system that I discovered that was over 1,000 years old, that was so highly developed, yet so simple and easy to apply. A system that worked. Why had this system been kept secret? Because it came from the former Soviet Union.

Russian Systema

Systema can be looked on as a martial art. But this entire system is a lot more. Systema has been taught for centuries in Russia and has only recently, at the end of the Cold War, become available in the West. Practitioners of this old art include, Mikhail Ryabko and Vladimir Vasiliev as well as Konstantin Komarov, Sonny Puzikas and Maxim Franz.

Observing how these Special Forces operators move and breathe is a revelation. Bodyguards in the West have always looked to the East for the truth in Martial Arts; Shaolin monks, samurai warriors, Kung Fu fighters, Tai Chi Chuan and Wing Chun masters. There is a long list of disciplines and philosophies. Yet right behind the Iron Curtain was a system of fighting, breathing and living as a warrior that was completely hidden to us in the West till the 1990's.

I have included as recommended reading "Let Every Breath, Secrets of the Russian Breath Masters" by Vladimir Vasiliev. Check out his web site for more information about his seminars, writings and DVDs at http://russianmartialart.com.

Discovering Systema was a revelation. Only in this Century are we beginning to understand the true significance of Systema and how it applies to bodyguard work.

Systema will continue to grow as it is understood in the West and it will have a huge influence on bodyguard training and methods. I cannot overstate how important Systema is to the Way.

This is one of the joys of training. Discovering new ideas (that are really very old) and new schools of thought and movement.

So here I repeat, you have to keep training, be it with firearms, edged weapons, hand to hand or other skills, like languages, security driving or cooking or plain old verbal skills.

Cooking? You ask? How do you survive during long shifts with limited access to good food and other cooking facilities in a fast moving environment? How do you fuel yourself? I once worked a detail in Africa with a former Secret Service agent who told me a story about how he was sent with a large advance team to an Eastern European country ahead of the President. They worked for over 18 hours without food. No one had provisioned for meals, let alone snacks.

We operate on fuel; food and liquid. Once we run out of our reserves, bad things can happen, as it did on that advance. "The Seven Ps Principle" applies here. Prior Proper Planning Prevents Piss Poor Performance. Please. If all other planning fails, having a granola bar or some high protein or calorie snack in your pocket can get you through a long foodless shift. And if you are given an opportunity to throw together a quick meal, seize it and feed your team as well.

That particular Secret Service detail must have been missing a Marine Gunny. I work with a Gunny who always seems to come up with solutions to impossible problems. He has taken the "adapt, improvise and overcome" mantra to perfection in the civilian world. He would come back with hot meals for everyone, having talked a local kitchen into producing the food, probably for a few lapel pins or other trinkets. He has produced a front-end loader out of nowhere to dig huge earthworks that would have had to have been dug with shovels. He has procured boats, planes and large limousines seemingly out of thin air. Maybe no one can understand his soft sing song Brazilian American accent but he always produces results. Even conjuring up a tiny field stove in a luxury hotel room to make sublime Cuban coffee at dawn.

We do not always have Gunny to work his magic, so for us mere mortals we have a saying, when you have an opportunity to eat, you eat, or if you have the opportunity to go to the bathroom, you go. It doesn't matter if you are not quite hungry or do not need to go. You will sooner or later, so you seize the opportunity when you can.

Timing in this business is everything and your time is not your own, it belongs to your Protectee.

ABILITY TO MAKE LASTING NETWORK CONTACTS

Call them associates, fellow bodyguards or professional allies, but unless you network, network, and network you will never get an endless stream of bodyguard jobs.

Every time you work is an opportunity to develop contacts and make a lasting positive impression on the people you work with. Building and nurturing relationships is part of the Way of the Bodyguard. It is not about just having names and cell phone numbers, it is more about having a quality relationship with particular individuals who you have worked with, who know who you are and how you handle yourself and who can vouch for you for additional jobs. Just as you can recommend them for any jobs or contracts that are offered to you.

Attending a reputable Bodyguard training school means you get to network with the best. At least, they will tell you they are the best. And you will hear over and over again that marketing yourself is important. If you look the part, and you know your stuff, have graduated from a few classes with the right skills, and more importantly you have won great contacts, you will get the job.

To get the job, you have to make an impression, immediately.
How immediately? Fifteen seconds?
How about five seconds?

Chapter Five

The Five Second Impression

You thought you had fifteen seconds. But it's more like five. It is never easy making a second impression count. Only first impressions seem to last. We instinctively make our minds up based on a number of psychokinetic factors (code for "I can't explain it"). If you want a scientific explanation read Malcolm Gladwell's "Blink." The book is in the Way of the Bodyguard Reading List. You need to know why you have to make so many split second, or five-second decisions in a sometimes dangerous and oftentimes tedious job.

The Interview and the Five Second Decision

What I do know when we are hiring new bodyguards, regardless of what their resume looks like is that those first five seconds count. I'll let you into a little secret. The resume is a guide, a prop I hold in my hands but it doesn't mean much. I've seen SEALS who have amazing resumes but fail to impress in an interview. And here is as good a place as any to explain why. Some Special Forces (SF) individuals are absolutely smashing at what they did in their SF career. They can jump out of planes at very high altitudes in faraway places and break and blow up stuff, but looking after people in civilized society and acting appropriately in high-class surroundings is an entirely different matter.

A few years ago, one of the greatest teams, at least on paper with their SF experience and training, assembled in a large Southern city for a low risk protection detail. They were super warriors, with stellar resumes we could all die for. However, after the detail ended, they decided to drink, and drink and drink. At about 3 AM rather than climb up the outside walls (which has been known to happen) they decided to see who could rappel down the elevator shafts in their suits, the fastest. They did not execute these tactical moves quietly. Hotel guests were awoken. Hotel management was called. Their hiring agency got involved. They were banned from the hotel and the agency never hired them again. The owner of the agency swore he would never hire "snake eaters" again. Now you would want these guys to be by your side in an overseas firefight because they would be the best of the best, but in a five star, okay maybe a three star hotel, you want a different approach. There is blowing off steam and then blowing up steam.

In another age, before political correctness was invented, you could have a three-day and night non-stop party in a penthouse of a very expensive hotel, paid for with the blessing and the vehement admonition of the Protectee who had left the country. He had prepaid for the penthouse, the girls, the drinks, the food and given a generous tip for the staff who were to pander to the partying bodyguards. That sort of behavior was condoned and paid for and did not involve the public. But taking celebratory and violent behavior out into the public arena and embarrassing the Protectee and the hiring agency is taboo. Getting a bad reputation in this business can happen very quickly. Social media, cell phone videos and lightning fast communications have put a damper on such out of control "wheels up" parties.

There is a place for all talents in this business. Which means the civilized civilian with many social and verbal skills and a strong physical presence and good bodyguard skills can find work, regardless of a lack of SF credentials and a DD214.

How to survive the interview

There are other books and articles about getting hired for an ordinary job. Being a bodyguard and following the Way, is not ordinary. Getting hired for a bodyguard job is different. There is a risk of conflict, mental and physical, or high stress, countered by boredom and low pay. The boredom can extend for hours, days, months. I do not think any other profession has such long hours. So an interview for a bodyguard job is different compared to applying for a job as a sous chef, bookkeeper or warehouse worker.

Briefly, for any hiring process there is a certain formula. The resume gets emailed and if accepted, the phone interview is conducted. Then if you pass the phone test, there is the personal interview by the agency. This could be followed by more interviews. The client and or the Protectee can get involved. Then there is the requisite background check and the calling of references to verify the resume.

After the phone interview there is the live interview.

The telephone interview? After receiving a resume, a telephone conversation is still the best way to screen potential bodyguards. How do you sound on the phone? Can you listen, follow instructions and not repeat everything said? Can you make a connection with the person on the other end of the phone without being overly friendly, or self-serving? We all talk on the phone to strangers all the time, but how well can you project yourself so that the person on the other end of the phone wants to meet and hire you?

Walk in the door and it is all over

You will make your best impression in the first five seconds of contact. How you enter a room, how you carry yourself, how you present yourself, how you shake someone's hand, what you do with your eyes and feet. It's all over for the shrewd observer in the first five seconds.

You have to believe in yourself and project an air of confidence. This is very different from being arrogant and thinking you are irreplaceable. We are all ultimately expendable. There is always someone else to replace us and the shrewd Agency or client knows this.

Keep your dignity to yourself

Starting out in the bodyguard business, you might have to do some horrible jobs, earn your way up, earn your stripes, whatever you want to call it. Do not think you will go right to the top with a high paying job in just a few months?

In Florida, we start as private investigator Interns. There is a two-year apprenticeship as an intern, with a "CC License" before becoming a private investigator or bodyguard and acquiring a "C License." Before you get a CC License, you have to complete a 40-hour course and pass an exam. The State of Florida does not look upon full time bodyguard work as qualifying for a private investigator's license. As of this writing, of the 40-hour classroom training, only 3 hours is apportioned to bodyguard training. You have to do Investigation work or a lot of it, to qualify as a full time investigator. That breaks down over 2 years as 50 weeks times 40 hours a week equals 2,000 hours times 2 totals 4,000 hours. You can get a year's credit if you cross over or retire from other verifiable and approved investigative work, such as a full time detective in a police department. There are other exceptions, but being a patrol officer in a police department or an MP in the Army does not an investigator make, nor for that matter, a bodyguard.

Earning a little over minimum wage as a CC Intern doing surveillance under the most difficult conditions, can be trying, but you have to start somewhere. There is no room at the top for big egos and the untrained. But conducting surveillance provides valuable experience and a necessary foundation to follow in the Way. You cannot underestimate the power of learning surveillance and counter surveillance skills by accruing thousands and thousands of hours of such work. I am glad I have that experience behind me. It is hard work, always challenging and oftentimes frustrating.

Reputation and contact list

You are only as good as your reputation and your contacts in your smart phone.

Your name is everything in this business. It is a small world and certain people stick together. Guys like to work with their own. Recon works with Recon, SEALs with SEALs, Rangers with Rangers, and so on. You only trust and have confidence in people you know and have worked with or come highly recommended. Vouching for someone is a big deal because you are putting your reputation on the line for someone else. That said we all like to (or should) mentor. We like to train and help people whom we like and have confidence in. It's the American way. Passing on the knowledge. That's how our military was built. The FNG gets to prove himself, he is mentored and after various trials and tests, he becomes part of the team. If the FNG survives, matures and sustains himself, he gets to mentor the new FNG.

Get a Mentor, become a Mentor

Once you build your reputation, build your contact list. Sometimes taking a low paying job is worth it in the long run just for the networking opportunity and a chance for other people to see what you are like. But do not spend the entire time you are on that low paying job telling anyone who will listen to you that that is what you are doing. I have had to work with men who acted like that. Do you think they were invited back?

In the real world, there are bodyguards who might not be the best but have the contacts, a bigger contact list than you. They can be busier than you for this simple reason.

What can you do? When you see guys less qualified than you getting better higher paying jobs? Network and train more. You need more contacts.

Once you get higher up the chain and get a reputation, you can find good people who are just getting into the business and groom them, mentor them. Of course some will try to steal your clients but if you are careful you can hire, train, and mentor upcoming bodyguards. This is a competitive business but we have to encourage new quality professionals.

Confidence versus Arrogance

One of the characteristics of men who carry guns for a living and have a lot of testosterone is that they think they are the very best in the protection industry. Now it is good to have confidence and have a very good opinion of yourself. But you have to be realistic and so many men are not. They have no idea how they look or appear to the outside world.

Would you hire yourself for this job?

One technique trainers use, be it telemarketers or bodyguard trainers is the mirror technique. "Stand in front of a mirror and look at yourself. Would you hire yourself for this job?" Of course, for the uninitiated, the unaware, they have no idea what they project to the outside world. Their answer, after looking at themselves is: "Hello good looking! I want to hire you right away! Lets get busy!" But we all cannot be Austin Powers.

The Art of the Interview

Our core bodyguard team arrived in a new city with a large family. We were told at the last moment before boarding the two chartered jets (a 747 and a smaller Airbus 320) that we had to fire all our current and very accomplished bodyguards.

Of the twenty bodyguards, only three of us were to travel to the new city. We had to hire a large number of bodyguards in a very small time frame in a city we had never worked in before. Local referrals soon dried up. We were scraping the bottom of the barrel but we didn't know which barrel. How did we do what we did in under 24 hours? The interviews were usually 10 to 20 minutes but we made our minds up in 5 seconds. Initially, we thought it was 15 to 20 seconds, but after comparing notes, we realized we made our initial and what turned out to be our final decision much faster.

Our reaction to the interviewee was always immediate, because we either liked whom we saw or we did not. The two of us conducting these interviews used a code, a discreet hand signal to show if we liked the person or not for the job, although we could usually tell what the other was thinking anyway. One of the benefits of working with really good bodyguards is that you know what they are thinking sometimes before they do themselves. Then we tried to mess with each other by giving funky hand signals. The results were always the same. We either liked him and thought we could hire and train him, or we could not.

If you have ever played music in a group, or trained with a cohesive tactical unit and taken direct contact in intense engagements, you know what the others you are close to are thinking and what they are going to do next. That is how great jazz groups improvise together. Or well trained SWAT teams or Special Forces teams work together. It is the same with bodyguards who work together a lot.

During the interview process, if we were unsure about a particular person, we rejected him. It is always the unsure ones who will cause trouble later, or sooner. The old adage if you have doubts, don't do it, applies to interviews as well. If we had doubts about someone or they had said something later in the interview that confirmed our initial uneasiness about them, well, that confirmed what we sensed right away. Don't hire him!

Unit Integrity

In a jazz band they would call it being in the swing, in a Marine fighting unit, unit integrity, and you cannot get a better name for such intuitive action oriented cohesion borne of long experience, trust, hard work and unerring street sense. We call it knowing what the other bodyguard is thinking and knowing how they are going to act, so you all perform as a unit. In some cases, I have made do without radios (for various reasons be it no equipment, dead batteries, poor reception or too loud an environment) when working with a select group of bodyguards. We know what the other was thinking and we had a sense of what would happen next and what we all had to do. There was nothing psychic or cosmic about such behavior, we were just used to working with each other. You could not do this with FNGs!

This is the same matching behavior that works between us during an interview. We know what the other interviewer is thinking. Now if the interviewee picks up on this, if he is that sensitive and can appreciate what we are doing, and plays along and displays such sharp instincts, well, he is hired on the spot.

Walking through the door

Back to the poor interviewee, as he walks through that door. First he has to find the door, not a Herculean task but you would be surprised at how many men have a poor sense of direction. Ask their wives or girlfriends.

We look to see how the interviewee walked through the door, how he presented himself to us and how he shook our hands. That took up more than 5 seconds and we had made up our minds by then. It seems flippant but if you do this enough, that is hundreds and hundreds of times, you develop an uncanny knack of figuring out who is employable for a particular job and who is not.

We place the chair the interviewee will be forced to sit in, as it is the only vacant one in the small room, in such a way that he cannot see all of us. He is exposing his entire body. No matter how he sits we can read his body language: how he moves his legs and feet, what he does with his hands, how he maneuvers his back and spine. We can read him like an open book and he has not even opened his mouth yet.

Sometimes, we would let him start the conversation. We would remain silent and wait for him to lead.

Why do we, the interviewers, have to talk in the interview? He is on display, on trial, as it were. We want to hear from him. How does he act under scrutiny? How does he act in situations that are not threatening but unusual and uncharted? We are not selling our vacancy. He is selling himself.

The new interviewee is struck with how at ease the two interviewers are in the room. He has been purposefully placed in the only available chair. It is not comfortable and it is not positioned so he can see all of us clearly. Does he pick up the chair and adjust it, so he is at ease? Does he try to exert control of his environment? Or what little he has control of? Then he has to endure this silence, until it is obvious he should be the one to begin the conversation. How does he begin? Does he demonstrate grace under pressure or is he a little defensive? Or is he offended? As if we are playing a game on him? Heavens! Why would we do such a thing? Is he easily upset? How much pride and ego does he exhibit?

His questions will reveal what he is thinking: the conditions, the hours, what is required of him, the pay, the way he is treated, interacting with the Protectees? If he thinks of all the details, we can see he has some experience in these matters. It is a strange combination we are looking for, a quick thinking individual able to follow orders but able to be creative while still being part of a cohesive team. We are looking for someone who is patient and unflappable, but able to act quickly in unusual circumstances.

The rest of the interview

Despite the five second decision, we can be wrong. We can be conned and we can be fooled. No system is perfect. For that reason, we have a fairly structured interview after he runs out of questions to ask. We run through his resume and look for red flags. We ask him whom he knows, if he has worked other bodyguard jobs and whom he has worked with and for agencies we are familiar with. We want to know how much training he has taken on and what he has done recently. We want to see his attitude to training, his openness to new ideas. We want to know a little about his personal life and what he does to relax after work. We are looking for mental stability and geniality. How does he think and how would he react to certain job specific tasks or challenges? We want to know how mentally agile he is, how responsible and mature he can be under trying circumstances. And what habits does he exhibit as a highly trained bodyguard?

Which begs the question, what are the most effective habits of the bodyguard? "Habits" might seem a little too psychoanalytic but these are acquired traits and trainable behaviors that make a bodyguard more desirable to be hired.

I have listed 10 but we could go on and on, however let's be realistic. The perfect bodyguard does not exist. We all have off days or off moments. We drift off into the white zone (see the next Chapter.) We keep striving for perfection, this is part of the Way, even if we never quite get there.

Chapter Six

10 Effective Habits of Successful Bodyguards

We have talked about qualities that a bodyguard has to possess. But what are the 10 most important habits that a bodyguard can demonstrate in his daily routine?

What can he reveal to demonstrate his competency, every day?

Here are the 10 essential habits

1. Arrive early.
2. Be prepared for anything.
3. Carry everything you will need immediately on your person, keep the rest in your car or Command Post.
4. Appearance and attitude are paramount - first impressions last. So dress the part.
5. Instincts rule but never assume.
6. Healthy mindset - prepare for the worst, enjoy the best.
7. Stay fit and in shape.
8. Loyalty and Integrity.
9. Network with other bodyguards and agencies.
10. Document everything.

1. Arrive early- Punctuality

If you arrive an hour earlier than expected you have time to get a feel for your situation, perform counter surveillance and generally get established with your new location. If you arrive a couple of days beforehand you really get established. Now that is going a little too far but with SF operations it is not unusual to arrive a few hours or days early to create a protective circle around a rendezvous point or a direct action that is planned. The SF team builds a hide, a hidden observation point in which to observe everything in the area of operation. They keep watch, make reports and wait. Thankfully as civilian bodyguards we get to wear nice clothes and do not have to dig our observation post, nor deal with ants and other bugs that bite and plastic bags you deposit your waste into. An hour early is enough, sometimes less is OK when arriving at your bodyguard job.

It depends on the mission, what you have to do and where. Let's take for example a hotel and a particular room you have to be in. Show up for a job five minutes before the start of your shift or arrive late and use "bad traffic" as an excuse, puts you in the amateur league.

Security guards show up 5 minutes before their shift starts. Bodyguards show up 30 to 60 minutes early. As a rule, show up early, up to an hour earlier, for your first day. Half an hour is usual once you get into a rhythm. For 12 hour shifts, realize the guy you are replacing has put in a full 12 hours and wants to go home or to his hotel bed. Arrive earlier and show him some respect. Replacing a bodyguard who has endured a boring 12 hour shift half an hour or an hour early will really help you build your own image. He will be in your debt and repay you in kind. (You hope.) Building respect and demonstrating a strong work ethic is vital to getting that next job. If you were SF it would have been arrive early and kill everyone. Now, it is arrive early and greet everyone.

2. Be prepared for anything

Mental preparation is everything. Our profession has been described as 80% preparation, 19.999% waiting and .001%

terrifying action. Well for some of us it is exciting not terrifying. But you get the point. To be a bodyguard you need a particular mindset, a winning mindset, an attitude that you will dominate, win and come out on top, with your Protectee's life and well-being coming first. Do not drift off into the white zone and blank out.

In the white zone? Jeff Cooper invented and perfected principles that today seem as fresh and relevant as when he first wrote about them. He taught modern America how to shoot, how to think about defensive tactics, how to categorize our states of awareness and a lot more. I teach his four principles of Firearm Safety as the Holy Grail of how to handle a firearm and the responsibilities entailed in possessing a firearm.

In my firearms class I say, "This will change your life forever. You will handle a firearm safely and you will look upon how other people handle firearms differently. It will change how you view guns in movies and how actors handle guns. And a word to the wise about seeing such gun handling mistakes, don't shout at the TV, your partner will get upset."

Here are Jeff Cooper's Four Gun Safety Rules as taught by yours truly.

1. All guns are always loaded all the time. Always. There are no exceptions. This means you can never say "Oh I didn't know it was loaded!" Idiot! All guns are always loaded all the time. Did I repeat always? I get the class to chant this over and over like, if they can remember, their multiplication tables. It does not matter if the gun is loaded or not, you treat every gun as if it is loaded.

When I went shopping for a hunting rifle in New Zealand, a young man in a large rambling country house took a rifle off the wall and said, "Look at this, it's a great rifle. It's not loaded." He pointed the muzzle right at my face and began to pull the trigger. I grabbed the barrel and twisted the gun out of his hands before he could complete squeezing the trigger. I pushed the rifle so it pointed upwards. It was a one-storey house. Refer to rule number 2. I then racked the bolt back and out popped a live round that did not, thank goodness, have my name on it. He was a little embarrassed. Embarrassed is an understatement. He was seconds from blowing my brains out because he assumed the gun was not loaded. I walked out of that house in one piece, with a newly acquired and unloaded rifle at a very attractive price. You always check a gun, even if you have just put it in your safe and know it was put away unloaded. Or you have just put it on the table and you know you have unloaded it, you check it when you pick it up again, and you check it again. The more you handle firearms and the older you get, the more fanatical you become about gun safety. You cannot be too fanatical about gun safety.

2. Never point a gun at something you do not want to destroy.

The cute way of saying this is always point your gun in a safe direction. At the range that means down range only, and not pointing the muzzle at your partner or someone else at the range. And tactically it means never pointing it at someone on your side even if the muzzle just points, (covers) a part of that person. Look at how SWAT teams stack up. No one has a muzzle pointing at anyone else. They all keep their firearms pointed "sol," south, downwards and their firearms do not cover or come into contact with others in the team. Just understanding this one rule will ruin your enjoyment of cop TV shows and a lot of films with guns. You can tell which actors have put in the time to learn correct gun handling skills and have spent time shooting and controlling their firearm. Constantly pointing out mistakes in gun handling by shouting at the TV, when sitting next to your significant other, will only cause that person to wish you were back on the road, on a long term bodyguard detail. "Look! He's holding it like a teacup! What does he think it is?" "Well, he's English. He drinks a lot of tea!"

3. Keep your finger off the trigger until ready to shoot.

What could be simpler? But check out all the film posters featuring women with guns, older versions of James Bond films and other action heroes. How many people demonstrate safe gun handling techniques? Ignorance and complete lack of firearm safety is celebrated by Hollywood in countless posters, DVD covers and other ads featuring the feckless actor holding a gun, usually upwards with his or her finger on the trigger.

4. Every bullet has an address.

You are responsible for every round you fire, every bullet that comes out of the muzzle of your gun. Once it leaves the barrel there is no turning back, it is on its way and better hit the target, not something or someone else. Fire a gun up in the air and the bullet will come down somewhere, that somewhere has an address. It could be the ground or a child's skull. Get my point? Or rather Jeff Cooper's. Be sure of your target, where you are shooting, and your surroundings.

Jeff Cooper also defined the color-coded system of awareness. Such a system will be discussed and demonstrated in any bodyguard school. It is illuminating to train through these codes and realize how you react to simple bodyguard situations in different colors. How your heart rate increases in each state and how your body responds. Here again training is critical to stress conditioning and stress inoculation.

The codes go from white, yellow, orange, red and then to black.

The colors match a state of awareness and heart rate;
White is unaware, very relaxed at 60-72 beats per minute.
Yellow is aware, and a normal heart rate of 72.
Orange is alert, with a heart rate over 115, and
Red is alarm, a heart rate rising over 145-175,
then we have Black. Your heart rate is zero. It has stopped.
When you are in the white state you are unaware, let's say you are daydreaming. This is not a good place to be when

guarding someone. Although we all slip into the white state occasionally on long tedious shifts.

Yellow is where we want to be most of the time. We are aware but relaxed. We are vigilant but not over reacting to the normal flow of life. There is nothing stressful happening but we are watchful.

Moving into an orange state means we are now in a heightened state of alert. Our heart rate is rising but we can still perform minor body movements and deal with the stressful situation.

When the heartbeats climb, and we can only perform gross body movements, we are in the red state. If we are not stress immune, things happen to our body we have no control over, our senses shut down and we focus down to the immediate threat. Have you tried dialing 911 in this red state? It can be very difficult, because all your fine motor skills have gone.

Then there is black. This is not a good color code to be in. Red has your heart racing. In black, your heart has stopped.

Jeff Cooper is a delight to read and "The Principles of Self Defense" is required reading in the list at the back of this book. Jeff Cooper's writing is straightforward, insightful, wise and did I mention he is a Marine. (My Editor wants me to change that verb to the past "was" but once you are a Marine you are always a Marine, you cannot be an ex-Marine, unless you are dishonorably discharged, you can only be a former Marine, but you are still a Marine. Even if you are in Marine Heaven, you are still a Marine, always. Did I mention I love hiring and working with Marines?)

Back to the yellow state. I might look like I am day dreaming and people will ask me if I am bored just sitting or standing somewhere. I have a saying: "If I am breathing, I am not bored." Enjoy breathing in the yellow state.

What if? exercises

How to keep from slipping into the white state and complacency

One trick I execute to keep myself alert is running through a number of scenarios that might happen where I am stationed. I game play every situation I can think of as in "What if such an event happened? What if this person came up to you? "And so on.

If I am with someone else, I can drive him crazy with these questions. It turns into a great time mover and learning experience. The "What ifs?" can be everyday encounters, or they can turn into unpredictable situations with unpleasant outcomes.

One banal example I've seen go both ways

I am posted on a hotel floor outside the Presidential Suite in a five star hotel in Beverly Hills.

"What if a man in overalls comes down the corridor. You've never seen him before and he has something large and metallic in his hands and he is not smiling. He looks angry. What do you do?"

Answer: Draw down on him and yell at him to drop the weapon and hit the ground.

Wrong. He is an engineer for the hotel. It was his day off. He had to drive to the hotel and fix a broken sink in your Protectee's Presidential suite. He was pissed off before he encountered you. Now he is really pissed off.

Answer: Smile and walk up to him, blocking his way but in a non-threatening way. The smile and greeting disarms him and allows you to see what he has in his hands. He knows who you are and informs you of his mission and you help him to the correct door. (Of course he knows who you are, don't you think bodyguards who are stationed in a hotel are the talk of the hotel staff?) You exchange names and feelings about being where you are and where you would rather be. (Do I have to go into the finer points?) He has a master key on his ID key chain and you have just made another friend. You walk in with him just to make sure he is not disturbing anyone and nothing funky is happening behind those closed doors. All the time you are helping the engineer, making his job easier, not harder. And now you have his cell phone number so you can call on him, when he is on his shift, to help you out if needed. The more friends you have in the hotel, the easier your job will be.

A not so ordinary example but as dramatic as it usually gets

A casually dressed young man with a camera gets out of the elevator – the same Presidential suite floor.

You approach him, inform him that this is a closed floor and you thank him for leaving. He tries to counter with a list of arguments, all spurious and you sense he is a reporter or paparazzi, anything but a lost tourist. You do not touch him (he could charge you with assault) but you are firm and say as little as possible while getting him onto the elevator.

We all have our own personal style in handling such situations as unwanted intruders in private areas. Yes, you did inform him this is a private hotel and no he has no right to be there. He is not in a public place and he does not have a constitutional right to be there. But you did not over react or somehow freak him out with too much verbal and physical presence or the use of physical force. All you did was avoid a serious confrontation or a breach of your security barrier, you were low key and professional, and did not do anything that would reflect badly on your Protectee.

3. Carry everything you will need immediately on your person, keep the rest in your car or at the Command Post. Be prepared for just about anything

Once you are mentally prepared, you have to be physically prepared. A new bodyguard detail always contains many unknowns. Most bodyguards are tool and gun freaks. We love buying new stuff, trying it out, breaking it and using what we can trust and feel comfortable with. You can never have enough equipment, unless you are carrying it up a mountain or across a desert for days. Better to have it and not need it than need it and not have it. The Protectee is always impressed when you pull out from nowhere some vital little item they so desperately need and you just happen to have, because you are a professional and have planned for everything. Like an emery board in your jacket pocket or a band-aid in your wallet or a small powerful flashlight.

There should be a list of equipment for certain types of jobs that you always have with you. What is the number one tool a bodyguard should carry? A flashlight. There are always dark places to light up. Fenix and Surefire are among an emerging number of brands that have small lithium battery Executive and Tactical flashlights that put out a blinding 200 + lumens for an hour. Get a couple and always have one or two on you. Know how to use it, as an illumination tool, as an intimidation and disorientation device, as a self-defense tool (some flashlights come with a mean looking crenellated bezel), and as a free hand light to go with your firearm.

Here is a list of equipment you should have on your person. I have operated with a bare minimum in a country where I cannot carry a firearm or a knife. Then I have operated in some nasty areas of the U.S.A. where I have extra high capacity magazines for my handgun and a shotgun (fully loaded) in the back of the car, just in case. When packing, always include extra ammo and a back up gun. There is no such thing as saying: If

I need more than 7 rounds then I am really in trouble. That is just incorrect. If you need even one round you are in trouble. And you will probably need a lot more rounds. When things go really wrong, you can never have enough time and you can never have enough ammo.

So I have compiled two lists. The bare minimum and the full Monty.

The Bare Minimum

For local work I would include one or two firearms (where legal and licensed to carry) and your cell phone, or two. I carry two cell phones, only because from bitter (not too bitter) experience, when you really need to use a cell phone, one of them is out of service.

You are right to question if I carry two cell phones why not two guns?

SEALs have a saying "One is None and Two is One." Redundancy is built into their training and execution of direct action operations. The same redundancy can apply to cell phones, flashlights and more importantly firearms. With so many new small guns available, it is an easy decision to carry a micro 9mm or a smaller 380. A concealable mouse gun is better than no back up gun at all. Get shot with a 380 jacketed hollow point and see if you still think this is not an effective round if placed properly. Be assured that the guy who has a few 380 rounds in him, if he is still alive will probably be squealing a lot and will never refer to that small caliber handgun as a "mouse gun" again.

A review of police officers who have been shot after their primary weapon malfunctions, will show that they did not get a second chance if they could not immediately transition to their second weapon.

Refer to the Way of the Bodyguard Reading List: "Violent Encounters: A Study of Felonious Assaults on Our Nation's Law Enforcement Officers." Force Science News at

ForceScienceNews.com also lists some very compelling research regarding force-on-force encounters equally relevant to professional bodyguards and high-risk encounters with firearms. These research papers make sober reading and I repeat, one is none, two is one.

Strong Belt

A double-sided leather belt can carry equipment, like cell phones, a gun, spare magazines and flashlight, without folding.

A small first aid kit (attached to your belt) should include such small items as Imodium pills, Tylenol, band-aids and alcohol swabs.

Multi purpose Tool (my mini Gerber has a knife but the handle is orange and it looks like an innocent tool)

Flashlight.

Tactical folders (two are better than one - if they are legal to carry).

Radio and ear piece (to communicate with the rest of my team).

Notepad and 2 pens.

Schedule and maps and any other Advance material prepared for the day's events.

Relevant licenses and other IDs.

The Bug Out Bag or the Go bag

Kiefer Sutherland made it famous, the brown nondescript shoulder bag he always carried in the FOX TV series 24. We call it a bug out bag or go bag and it contains just about anything you might need in an emergency, without being too big or heavy. Everyone in high risk businesses has one, or two, even if they keep them in their vehicle or office. Everything you might need at a pinch is in that bag and you keep adding to it as you buy or think of new tools. Make a list of your needs and always have the bug out bag around. There is no one list of things you have to have in this bag. Everything depends on your needs and mission.

I always have a bug out bag in my car. Even if I am not on the job, it is within reach. I keep in the bug out bag, an extra firearm, several fully loaded magazines, two different knives, two flashlights, a multi tool kit, pens, notepad, lots of spare batteries, another first aid kit including emergency wound care bandages, latex gloves, a CPR mouthpiece and a full range of small travel size over the counter medications. The bag is full and I add or rearrange the items depending on my tasks and needs.

If mobile and in another country, or an unfamiliar area, I always carry, when appropriate, a shoulder bag. It looks like a harmless students shoulder bag, as I do not want to draw attention to the bag or myself. It is not a black tactical operators kit, but it is filled with first aid equipment and every conceivable over the counter medication and pill and bandage and other pharmaceutical item I can think of, including emery boards. I also manage to squeeze in some granola bars and other non perishable individually wrapped and sealed, high calorie snack foods, enough for the entire team, and small bottles of water, enough to last for 24 hours without a real meal.

The Works

In the U.S. I carry on my person:

A notepad and 2 pens.

Keys - with a small tool kit, handcuff key and a few other items on a key chain including a blue LED light.

ID - Florida State requires I carry my C and G Licenses, also my Concealed Weapons Permit, and other licenses - of course Drivers License, Agency ID, auto insurance and registration, medical insurance and so on. I need two wallets - one for official IDs and my business cards and one for personal IDs, credit cards etc.

I have a badge. I can put it on my belt or on a neck chain or in a special wallet. I can show it to police if the situation arises. Such as when the arriving police officers do not know who is who. If you have a badge, chances are they will think twice about shooting or tasering or pepper spraying you. You will have gained a few seconds to tell them you are a good guy. You are there to help and follow their instructions.

If you do have a badge, bear in mind you are not a cop and should not give the impression however unintentional, that you are one. Keep the badge hidden and do not place it on your belt for all to see.

A note on the Federal badge law, the Enhanced Federal Security Act of 2000 states that you cannot wear or use a police badge or one that resembles a police badge if it would deceive an ordinary individual into believing it was a real police badge. Florida State has a similar law in Statute 493. We call it "the 20 foot rule." If a reasonable individual can make out that it is not a police badge from 20 feet, you are OK. Both State and Federal laws are rather subjective and you do not want to rely on the interpretation of an officer who is having a bad day. Don't show the badge. You are a bodyguard, not a cop. Viva La Difference. That said I have found a lot of cops respect you if you "flash them your tin," having a badge and the confidence to show it, makes them feel less wary of you. It all depends on the situation, how you comport yourself and how they are feeling.

Confused? You should be. Cops can be too. I have been told to get out of my car at gunpoint by a cop. Then he wants to see my badge. I show him my badge and he is OK. He puts away his gun and talks to me as if I am a professional. Do I lecture him on the fact that he needs to really see my Licenses and other IDs? No. I am thankful he is no longer yelling at me and pointing his gun at me. Other times on static details in rich neighborhoods I have had every patrol cop on a particular shift drive by and demand to see every single license I have on me. That is OK too. They are being thorough and I am acting professional. Never get into a pissing match with a cop who is doing his duty. He can ruin your day. He can arrest you. Tact, charm and a calm demeanor can go a long way in defusing a situation that only starts with a simple misunderstanding. Do not go toe to toe with a cop. You have the power to piss him off. He has the power to arrest you, put you in handcuffs, until his supervisor comes along to straighten things out.

Weapons: I am certified to carry a 9mm. Hmmm, I no longer like that term: "I am certified to carry," because it reminds me of that famous video clip of a DEA agent shooting himself in the leg after he thinks he has safety checked his Glock, in class. Lets just say I carry an appropriate firearm for the job I am about to do. For years, I carried a Glock. Then I switched to a Sig Sauer 228. Now I am back with a Glock. Does this make any sense? No, but I get to shoot a lot of guns.

This is not a discussion on what is the best gun to carry. I have also had a small 380 hidden in my back pocket. For the record, my favorite gun is the one I have with me. Everyone has their individual preferences, what they shoot best. In Florida, we can carry 9mm, 38 Special, 380 and now 40 and 45 caliber handguns, under our G Statewide Firearm Licenses. Other States have different requirements and restrictions.

I have high capacity magazines. I have two extra magazines on my belt. For low risk jobs, that is 51 rounds plus one in the pipe. I always top off the magazine in my handgun. In a shooting investigation, it is standard operating procedure to assume that the shooter did top off his magazine. NYPD and other police departments will look for that extra ejected casing after a shooting. Your job is always about reducing risk, being prepared and taking as many precautions as possible under the circumstances. That extra round is important. Why do actors rack their semi automatic pistols just before they go into action? That racking sound drives me crazy! You can safety check your firearm at the appropriate time, but that means you already have a round in the chamber. You just want to confirm that and that the magazine is securely in place. If you have done enough firearms training, you will know that extra round could be needed.

For high-risk jobs, I carry more magazines, a lot more. A quick magazine story here just to demonstrate you can never have enough magazines. A good friend and a highly respected firearms instructor had built in magazine holders in the side of his car doors, he had extra magazines in his desk, by the front door, in his house they were on top of picture frames by the front door and next to his bed. You get the picture. He had a lot of magazines all over the place, but especially on or near his person. He is a very sane person and in no way a fanatic. He just has lots of common sense, and spare magazines.

I also carry another gun. If Texas Rangers carry three, I can carry two. Three you ask? That would be one in a strong side holster, one in a side or rear pocket and one clipped to a cowboy boot. I do not wear cowboy boots but they are great for hiding small guns and knives.

You can always have more ammo and guns in the car, readily available. I have a gun safe or two in my car, hidden of course. I keep a trunk gun with an extra magazine, hidden, where else but in the trunk, in a safe, that is bolted to the car body.

The holster you wear is vitally important. You should be able to draw your gun without covering (pointing at) anything or anyone else. At the same time, the gun should be able to be retained in a fight or if you fall over or leap over a wall. Can you stand upside down and the gun stays in place? All weapons, all equipment you carry, has to be fight proof, to be able to survive a tussle on the ground, or a crowd pushing and pulling you.

Strong side belt holsters are the best. Either inside the waistband or looped through the belt or paddle. You can quickly re-holster your firearm with one hand while keeping the other open. You cannot do such a re-holster with a James Bond type shoulder rig. Yes, they look fancy and might be the only option in a dinner jacket with a cummerbund but they are impractical most of the time. And when drawn, the muzzle tends to cover half the people in the room. Not good manners or sound gun safety.

I always have my flashlight, even during the day. There are always dark places to illuminate and you want to use batteries not bullets. Better to illuminate and intimidate than eliminate. Yes, I confess, I made that up but you have no idea how many people I come across who work at night and do not carry flashlights. Every good bouncer or nightclub security worker lives by his flashlight, or two. If you carry a gun and work at night, how are you going to shoot accurately? Are you going to wait for the correct light to illuminate the threat?

The FUBAR Card

Here is a happy piece of information you need to carry, what I call the FUBAR Card. Just in case. (For non-military readers, FUBAR stands for F'ed Up Beyond All Recognition. This means you.) What if something happens to you and no one knows who you are or what you are? Yes, you have your licenses and IDs. They are in your wallet but what about the vital information about yourself. This includes your name and address, phone numbers, next of kin, or person responsible for you, blood group, insurance card and so on. It is amazing how many security guards keep such material in their car or at home. You can also put this in your cell phone under ICE, short for In Case of Emergency, a list of emergency contacts to call from your cell phone. No one ever wants to get one of these calls, but it is preferable to be notified earlier rather than later. This includes your insurance card as well, for if you are injured or unable to communicate with emergency personnel, they need to find your insurance card. Do you know how many people I have seen die because the rescue personnel could not determine if the injured person had insurance and what Emergency Room (ER) they were to transport this person to? OK, so it is not a large number but you do not want to be one of those statistics. If all the ERs are full, where are they going to take you if you do not have verifiable medical insurance? If it's a full moon and county payday, all the ERs will be full. Here in South Florida we have an amazing Trauma One facility. But other regions might not be so egalitarian in their emergency dispatch.

Communications gear

This includes a smart cell phone, as well as a radio and earpiece to communicate with others in your team, call list or call codes. I have two cell phones from different cell phone networks as I find that one doesn't always work when I really need it. At least one cell phone has to be smart, internet enabled so I can look up information on the web, make bookings, find maps and directions, and retrieve information immediately. It is also email capable so I am always in touch and can communicate with other members of the team either by radio, cell phone, texting or email.

One thing I never do is use my phone when I am with the Protectee unless under his direction for some specific task such as summoning the driver.

Where is the driver?

You do not want to hear that question, where the driver has been given ample time to get to the predetermined spot. We arrive with the Protectee and find no vehicle, no driver.

There is always opportunity for on the job training. A few drivers seem to lack that one human ingredient that is so essential to bodyguards: common sense. As the saying goes, it is not too common.

For a driver I have not worked with before, I like to give him a one-page document that outlines what he should do. The one page is like a "Standing Orders" if he has had a military background. I do not want to offend his ego or sensibility, but nevertheless I stress that he has to make the Protectee happy and that a happy Protectee will tip better. This stick and carrot approach can come back to bite you, if you will excuse the mixed metaphors. But this is not the Way of the Driver. I could talk all night about driver stories, hilarious in hindsight but at the time almost catastrophic for the Protectee. There are many well trained security drivers and experienced limousine drivers who know how to act in appropriate company. It is that one unthinking driver who will provide entertaining stories for many a long shift. That said, in my experience female drivers seem to be different and have always been keen to learn, can listen and perform much better than their male counterparts.

In your car or at the Command Post

Here is a list of everything you should have in your car. There are other items to add as well, depending on the mission.

First Aid Kit.

I have collected and built up an extensive first aid kit as well as every over the counter drug, pill, lotion and type of Band-Aid. I have hot and cold bandages for sprains, ACE bandages, a full blown Trauma Kit with bloodstopper and huge strips of gauze, gloves, wipes, and just about everything but an AED. (If you are transporting an older executive an AED is important, especially if you are in his vehicle).

Really critical here are lots of gloves and a CPR shield or two. You can build up your own first aid kit. I keep it in a non-descript shoulder bag. I do not want to walk into a Protectee's house carrying a huge red bag with a black cross on it. This can alert the Protectee that perhaps he really is in danger. Better to be low key and subtle. Disposable gloves - you can never have too many - the Nitrile, blue slash resistant kind are the best. I keep extras in my car's glove compartment together with a CPR shield. Everything is sealed in clear plastic bags so I can see what I have.

Whatever you think you might need, put it in your car. Making a couple of trips to the trunk is better than being stuck for hours in the wrong place, with the wrong gear, or no gear at all. I keep a large collection of maps, a change of clothes, binoculars, cameras, extra radios and ear pieces, spare batteries, another cell phone charger, and of course an ice box - really a large canvas bag with food and drink, a box of wipes so I can keep my hands clean and some large garbage bags, I call them body bags but they do come in handy. Always have lots of water on hand and granola bars or some snacks that do not melt in the heat.

Change of clothes is important to have. Whether you transition from casual to formal or from a sports event to a banquet, a bodyguard has to be prepared for unexpected and new situations. You always have to look the part.

4. Appearance is paramount

First impressions count. You arrive early and you are dressed appropriately. Meticulously groomed. Perhaps a little smarter than expected. If the dress code calls for suit and tie do not show up in Dockers with a sports jacket, a wrinkled shirt and a tie that looks like a napkin. Shoes must always be shined and immaculate even if you wear tactical boots. Hair must be sharp, neat, regardless of length, it has to look well trimmed. You can have long hair and look like Antonio Banderas or you can have a shaved head or a crew cut. Just look like a million dollars not like you have come from another 12 hour shift. And always shave. The grubby unshaven terrorist look does not impress. You are not auditioning for a 90's music video. If you are meticulous about your appearance you are sending out other signals as well, especially to bad guys; that you care, that you are alert and that you can react quickly to any situation.

Do you think I am making this up?

A landmark five year study was conducted by the FBI in a 180 page summary called "Violent Encounters: A Study of Felonious Assaults on our Nation's Law Enforcement Officers." This was the third study conducted by FBI researchers. The first two were; "Killed in the Line of Duty (1992) and "In the Line if Fire" (1997).

In their first study, cop killers were interviewed in prison. The number one reason why the prisoner thought he could take on the cop was because the cop was dressed sloppy and the cop looked unprofessional. The cop killer's assessment was self-fulfilling. They were correct, because they were alive but in prison, while the cop was dead. This is why officer presence is the first line of defense in the Force Continuum models most States employ for their officers. Officer presence translates for us to bodyguard presence.

This is why Bodyguard Presence is so important.

The cop killers, would say phrases like:

He wasn't paying attention.

It was like a 9 to 5 job for him.

He seemed very lax, very bored.

He had his shirt sticking out and he looked unaware, I thought I could take him on.

His shoes were dirty and his belt was hanging off his fat gut.

He looked too fat to be a cop.

He looked easy. He was badly dressed.

His hair was mess, he just looked lazy, I could take him.

He wasn't prepared to take me on.

You get the picture? Have you ever looked like this on the job? Would you hire someone who looked and acted like this?

Officer presence is the first concept taught to police recruits in their officer safety and use of force course. If you do not have a presence, you are already behind in the first part of your encounter with someone who could hurt you. That is why you see rookies with their specially cut short sleeves shirt showing off their biceps, their short military style haircuts and sharp polished shoes. They look sharp. Their message is clear: don't mess with me. I've got it together and I can whip your ass. For bodyguards, you do not have a badge or other police to back you up. But that does not mean you have to wear specially tailored tight short-sleeved shirts to show off your biceps. In many situations, being low key is a better approach. As a bodyguard, you do not have arrest powers. This is not the Way. The Way of the Bodyguard calls for a subtle and situational approach.

Bodyguard Presence entails more than dress and attitude. You do have to look the part, be presentable and alert, but there is something more here that a predator or someone who could threaten your Protectee would pick up on. A quality that would cause such an attacker to rethink what he was going to do. There are many such professionals out there who project this sense of calm control.

5. Instincts rule but never assume

Being in a State of Instinctive Awareness

Instincts can be honed by experience, but there is an indefinable quality that the best operators have. I have tried to articulate this, because it is more than so-called "street smarts." Having good instincts can be defined as when you can immediately read a situation and predict what will happen. You get a feeling about a place or situation and take preventative measures, a few seconds or minutes later you see what happens and you are prepared. Is this too abstract for you?

Here we go with another mundane example and if you are complaining that there are too many mundane examples and not enough daring and exciting adventures then you have the wrong idea about being a bodyguard and the Way. There are few exciting adventures that happen. Most of the bad things that happen on your shift are caused by either poor planning or by a visit from Mr. Murphy. Being a bodyguard is mundane, boring, tedious and predictable, most of the time. Just like the hotel corridor story at the beginning of this book, it takes brains, intuition and good training to get through each day, however challenging or ordinary your shift is.

Mr. Murphy you ask? Pray tell who is this Mr. Murphy? And have I read too many Richard Marcinko books? (See the reading list at the end of the book). Mr. Murphy, or Murphy's Law, is a way of saying if things can go wrong, then they will go wrong and it is usually at the worst possible time and place. Mr. Murphy usually interferes in most tactical and protection plans. That is why we conduct advances, plan for contingencies, and expect the unexpected. For example, that road trip you advanced last night to double check that your Protectee would be safely transported to his destination this morning, is now the subject of an elaborate road repair project and there are detours and traffic holdups that were not present yesterday.

I was introduced to Mr. Murphy early, in New Zealand. I was hiking in the bush with a friend. We got lost. Night fell. Our flashlights did not work. We had no more food or water for we had planned a day hike. And did I mention we were lost. "Well at least it's not raining." I said. Silly me. The heavens opened up and the entire forest flooded. We found the ranger's hut the next day and got out of the forest. Even today with GPS, hikers get lost in the New Zealand bush. Mr. Murphy turns up.

There is a Yiddish saying, "Mentsch tracht, Gott lacht." Translation: Man plans, God laughs. That Mr. Murphy laughs is open to question. He will visit though, when you least expect him.

So here is another common example, when two drunks collide.

You are at a popular bar. It is packed and noisy. You are surrounded by boisterous men and women who are drinking. You are working. You are sober. You may sip on a soda or water but are not feeling relaxed, even if you look relaxed. This is one of the worst environments to be in. Lots of people drinking lots of alcohol, what can go right?

The Protectee has already made it known he is not leaving for anything. There is an attractive girl he is chatting up. You have identified two threats, not assassins, more like annoyances: two drunks, one at each end of the bar. They are slowly working their way to the center where your Protectee is talking to a beautiful woman. Now the bodyguard schools would teach you that you have to pick up the Protectee and evacuate him immediately. That is Secret Service protocol in such a situation, but guess what? Secret Service would never have allowed their Protectee to be there in a noisy bar full of drunks in the first place. You are not Secret Service. You are alone in the private sector and the client does not want to be whooshed away, that would be humiliating for his Type A personality. And he would fire your ass.

An hour later the two drunks bump into each other and one tries to hit the other, arguing over the girl who is in front of your client. What do you do? You've had more than an hour to plan this out with all the "what ifs" that have been running through your mind as you sip your lemonade. You grab one of the drunks, the bigger one, before he can swing a punch and put him up against a pillar, your arms wrapped around his body pinning his arms. You whisper into his ear that he has to leave before something terrible happens to him. He does not appear to be listening to you because he is disoriented by your sudden and unexpected action. What happened to him? There is a knee pressing up against his private parts.

But you have bought some valuable time. Your Protectee is safe, perhaps he has not even noticed what has happened. Security arrives, as usual too late, and whisks him away. The three large men in black shirts know who you are because you introduced yourself to them earlier in the evening. They have the idea that you are in the same profession. The nod and shake of hands maybe even a tip earlier now pays off. They realize you are not a threat and leave you alone. You turn around and your client still has not noticed what you have done, he is too busy chatting up the girl. Welcome to the real world. Your intuition helped you identify and solve a problem and you did not assume anything. Do not expect a thank you from your Protectee, you were just doing your job.

Always verify, never assume. Assume makes an Ass out of You and Me, the saying goes. You never want to say to your client, I assumed it was OK. Because he will assume that he will fire you.

6. The Winning Mindset - Prepare for the worst, enjoy the best

With all the equipment, training and planning I have prepared for the worst. And the worst might be only that I am not fed on my shift. But I am prepared. I have a granola bar. It might be worse. I could need Imodium!

I have a reply to anyone who asks: Aren't you bored standing there all this time?

What I am really demonstrating is the Winning Mindset. What? You look half bored!

I am not bored, half bored or quarter bored. I am breathing, and happy. What can be better than nothing happening? I am being paid to make sure nothing bad happens. So I am never bored. If I looked bored, it is deceptive. Try and do something you shouldn't near me and see what happens.

The Winning Mindset is not some trait that springs to life in an instant, milliseconds before an epic battle with masked assassins who appear out of clouds of smoke. It is part of the Way of the Bodyguard, part of breathing, part of being a bodyguard.

There is an unwritten rule in this business; go to the bathroom whenever you can and eat and drink whenever you can, because these opportunities do not come regularly. You do not work in a union environment where you can take prescribed breaks. You cannot call dispatch and sign off for a few minutes for a break. The flow of events for your shift is usually unpredictable. So seize any opportunity you can or regret it later. Such breaks can be very irregular. Take for example traveling with a client who runs everywhere with no consideration for you. There will be instances where you are compelled to hold it in or be hungry or wish you had packed a snack in your pocket.

But if I have just eaten, have been to the bathroom, and I am standing somewhere and have no idea what is going to happen later because there is no schedule, well I am not bored, I am happy and I am enjoying the moment. Partially full stomach, empty bladder, Protectee happy nearby, no threats or logistic nightmares, what could be better? And I am getting paid. It usually does not get better than that. I am not content daydreaming or goofing off, for I still possess that Winning Mindset, that ability to spring into action if necessary, in a yellow state of awareness.

7. Stay fit and in shape

Personal Fitness and Hygiene

If you had to choose on the spot between two men to work with in a high risk assignment, how would you choose them? If one was out of shape, had a beer belly, unkempt hair, unshaven, bleary eyed and was smoking and the other who stood up straight, had a flat stomach and looked sharp, it would not be a hard choice would it? How do clients pick protectors? Not on looks alone, but physical appearance is important.

I have worked with enough Royal Saudi Families to know they have experienced and seen hundreds, sometimes thousands of bodyguards. As the Royal members mature they have a very good idea of who is good and who is not. Sometimes the Royal members can be fast in their selection or firing of bodyguards. They might employ their own version of the 5 second interview and instinctively decide whom they like or dislike.

The record is five minutes for one bodyguard. My second in command hired him for a team I was in charge of. I was out of town at the time and would not have hired him, but you work with whom you have available. One member of the Royal party took one look at him and said he had to go. He did not look the part. The Royal worker whom I managed to ask later, rather casually, what they did not like about my 5 minute bodyguard said simply. "I did not have a good feeling about him." There you have it in a nutshell.

Look in the mirror, again

Would you hire yourself? Imagine you are the Protectee and you see your own image. Would you feel safe hiring that person in the mirror? Now look at other bodyguards. Would you hire them to protect you?

The "what if "exercise goes like this: If I had been threatened and really feared for my life and had to hire a bodyguard (someone else was paying), whom would I hire? The possibilities of who to hire are reduced rather quickly. I would only have a handful of bodyguards I would select to protect me.

Coming of Age

All bodyguards eventually wear out. We might like to think we are indestructible but we are not. Sooner or later we will have to retire, there are few 60 plus year old bodyguards out there. If you are over 60 and still working, you must be really good and in shape. You cannot stop the clock. But you can slow it down and you can keep your reflexes, your joints and your entire body in shape by working out regularly.

You owe it to your team, your work mates, to stay in top shape, whether it is a 3 mile run every morning or a quick workout at night after your shift.

If you are not working it, you are losing it.

There is a computer geek saying: YMMV, Your Mileage May Vary. It goes for bodyguards as well.

But there are always exceptions or should I say anomalies.

While staying at a five star hotel and looking after a family, we often have to double up in rooms. Two bodyguards, two queen sized beds. The rooms are not suites, they are the cheapest available and sometimes there is a camp bed in there as well for a third person. This is where hiring recently demobbed

Marines or SF guys can come in handy. They are ecstatic to be sleeping in a camper bed or on the floor of a luxury hotel. They have never had it so good. Unlike some spoiled civilian bodyguards present company not included of course.

I am asleep in my shared hotel room when I am awakened at 3 AM by my new room mate who is practicing his Tai Chi routine right next to my bed, breathing hard and waving his arms and legs about. Now here comes the really weird part. He is stark naked. He is not an underwear model to start with. Underwear would have been good here. The belly hangs low, even if he has a large barrel chest. But the belly does not hang low enough and I can see in the low light, everything. He is naked! In front of me! That was not a pleasant awakening. At least only his Chi was rising as he breathed loudly, his eyes intensely focused on me.

I transferred him to another room the next day. Yes, I know, he gets full marks for working out in his hotel room so diligently, but not for waking me up and seeing his naked body in a Tai Chi pose over my bed.

The Tai Chi enthusiast did not have such a good roommate the next night. Was this karma? I hope not because he was a highly experienced and skilled bodyguard. We put him with the FNG. Only the FNG still lived with his mother. He was a local and he got to share a room as we kept long work hours. The Tai Chi man woke up to find the FNG in bed with a woman. Now there is etiquette and there is bodyguard etiquette but how can you sneak a girl into the room you are sharing with a work mate? The Tai Chi man, now suitably clad in pajamas did not sleep much that night. We fired the FNG the next morning and now ask interviewees if they live with their mother.

The Perfect Exercise Program

Just like my favorite gun is the one in my hand, my favorite exercise program is the one I can do right here and now.

Whether its using the hotel gym or swimming pool or going for a mind clearing run after a long shift or just a quick workout in the hotel room, suitably dressed and not waking up a sleeping co-worker, there are a lot of options.

I have lifted weights since I was 12 years old. Now I realize I get better results and feel healthier by utilizing easy but effective low impact high repetition bodyweight exercises. These exercises have been around for hundreds of years. And they work.

There are many conditioning programs out there that combine many centuries old techniques and exercises to build and maintain strength and stamina, speed and flexibility. Loren Christensen outlines many such exercises in his Solo Conditioning books. Let Every Breath, Secrets of the Russian Breath Masters by Vladimir Vasiliev and Scott Meredith, explains the basis of Systema and breathing. The exercises are deceptively simple but they work. (See The Way of the Bodyguard Reading List).

It is better to execute a 10 minute work out in your hotel room, 50 push ups, 50 sit ups, 50 leg raises, deep breathing, some yoga and stretching, than to just lie on your bed and channel surf.

A quick work out at the end of your shift invigorates you and you will sleep better. Which brings us to what could be our most important time as a bodyguard, sleeping. If you do not get proper sleep, you can always catch up on days off. I do not say adequate, there is the saying "I'll sleep when I'm dead." I prefer the saying, "I'll sleep when I have finished this job." Some jobs go on for months and we never seem to get a full nights sleep. Time to catch up after the detail is over.

Sleep sweet dreams

I keep on saying you can never do enough of this and that. One thing I can never get enough of is sleep.

If you are working in a stressful job and work out as much as you can, you need seven to nine hours sleep a day. Sleep helps you rebuild your body, rewire your brain and sleep allows you to dream and nourish your self for the next day, the next shift.

No one wants to work with a tired sleepy bodyguard on duty. Working long shifts you might only get 5 to 6 hours of sleep a day. Make it count and turn off the TV in your bedroom. You can catch up on your sleep between jobs. My favorite trick to get new jobs was to have a nap on my sofa in the afternoon. The phone would ring. I would get a new job offer. It was never a dream job but with long hours and an immediate start, how could I say no? These jobs might not pay that well, but I would never have a chance to spend any money as I would always be working. I would always take the job. It would be better than napping on my sofa.

8. Loyalty and Integrity

These are basic values in our profession. They are neither traits nor trainable qualities. They are core values. You either have them or you do not. You are loyal to your team, your Protectee, your partner. You do not gossip or back bite or spread rumors or talk out of turn about other people. You know when to keep your mouth shut and when to speak up.

You either have integrity or you don't, there are no half measures here.

Imagine if you start talking about someone you have worked with to new team members, guys you have just been introduced to, maybe it is an unflattering but hilarious story. What will they think of you? Imagine you are spouting off secrets to a new client to try to impress him. He will be thinking, what will you be saying about him behind his back?

You can learn ethics, you are born with integrity. You are either loyal to the people you work with or you are not.

I have worked with Secret Service men and none of them talk about each other. I have caught a few micro expressions over a certain person who claims to be a former Secret Service agent. But I have never gotten the story about this person and

I never will, because they never tell, they never gossip and they never tell tales. We can all learn from this example.

Avoid working with people who lack integrity. They will talk about you behind your back, steal your clients and poison your networks. What is a network? A social network of like minded bodyguards, employers, agencies, clients and potential clients and other sources.

9. Network with other bodyguards and agencies

Some bodyguards have a real talent for connecting with people and partying with them so they can connect with Protectees.

As in any business, an excellent marketer with poor skill sets of a bodyguard can make more money than a poor marketer who is an excellent bodyguard.

What can you do?

Network with the people you work with. Cultivate new relationships with new agencies and potential clients. A really good operator will be silver tongued, able to con maitre d's, concierges, and limousine drivers into doing what the bodyguard wants. That is the secret of a good advance man. Something you will learn in a good bodyguard school.

Here is one common mistake for new bodyguards. Do not give out your own business cards when working for another agency. That is not ethical. If someone is paying you for a job, do not go and represent yourself to others on their time. That business card you gave out will come back to haunt you. If someone does that to you once, he will do it again. Get rid of him immediately. He is not worth working with.

This has happened to me a few times. The worst case was when I was managing security for a celebrity funeral. I needed extra people and the owner of another agency I was close to then, swore that this new guy was perfect. Former marine, bodyguard for a high government official, graduate of one of the top bodyguard schools; he was personally vouched for by the owner. He was, however, the FNG.

After the funeral, the bodyguard for Michael Jackson handed me the FNG's business card. He knew this was the wrong thing to do so he let me know right away. At the bodyguard school this former marine graduated from, they taught you that you never gave out your own business card when working for someone else. It was a complete no no. Michael Jackson's bodyguard, being a well trained and ethical human being, knew this too. We all do. I confronted the FNG in front of his boss who had vouched for him and he made up a lie. Not a very good lie even, and he did not confess when confronted with his made up business card.

I never used him again. I found out later he had been dishonorably discharged from the Marines after only one year. So he was not a former Marine, he was an ex-Marine. Big difference.

Semper Fi. If the bodyguards you hire are not faithful what use are they?

10. Document everything - you can never have enough information. If it's not written down, it never happened

I keep a notebook and a couple of pens with me at all times and a tiny digital camera. Now this high-resolution camera is incorporated into a smart phone. But you get the picture, if anything odd happens that does not need your immediate physical attention you can take digital photos. Smart phones can document unobtrusively events that can be analyzed later. This applies to shooting crowds so you can look at the faces later. If you can show to your Protectee that the known stalker, or ex-employee or threat was in a crowd nearby, you have just extended your contract.

The same strategy of documenting who is around you, can apply to looking after celebrities and their mandatory stalkers. You are not a celebrity unless you have at least one person obsessed by you, who might appear at any time, in any situation.

Looking at these photos later, on a big screen can add to intelligence gathering and identification of known stalkers, paparazzi and other persons who interact with your celebrity and might not have good intentions.

A pen and pad should always be on you. I am still amazed when I give instructions or a phone number or address to another bodyguard and they do not have a pen and paper on them. What business are they in I wonder?

I love collecting tags, license plate numbers. A habit I got from doing bank robbery surveillance. Do you know how boring standing outside a bank can be for 10 hours a day with extended banking hours, in the hot sun, in a suit and concealed body armor and enough weaponry to take out a small Taliban army?

Remember I said if I'm breathing I'm not bored. Well, it's difficult to breathe with so much gear on, but I can take note of license plates and match the cars to the people as in "what is wrong with this scene?"

Let me explain. Part of my training program for bank robbery suppression, or any detail that requires spending time in a public area, entails memorizing faces and matching them to how they act, what they wear and the cars they drive and matching their cars to license plates. Anything out of the ordinary or that sets off alarm bells, gets recorded.

You have to recognize what does not seem right. These surveillance techniques work in hotel lobbies, shopping malls, any public space. There are always two tape loops running through a good bodyguard's head:

There are the "what if" scenarios? What if so and so walking up to me does that, what do I do?

And the other is: What is wrong with this picture?

Two men ease out of a new luxury car. They are dressed in old baggy clothes. One has a large shopping bag that appears heavy. They look around and seem nervous and out of place in the upscale parking lot next to a bank. The one without a shopping bag has a large waist pack. Not all "pictures" are this obvious and many have different outcomes to what you might first expect. They had parked their car facing in, so they could not make a quick getaway parked as they were further away from the bank. They were both going into the bank. There was no getaway driver.

The two badly dressed men walk up to the bank. I had already approached them in the parking lot and said, "That looks heavy. Everything alright? We are security here."

In that quick micro encounter, three things were going on. I was telling them I knew they were up to something, I was offering my help and I was telling them who we were so if they were good guys (which I sensed they were, as they were too old for bank robbers, although you can never be too sure, hence my friendly mock casual manner).

My partner was standing to one side as back up. He did not know what was going on and was trying to catch up on the OODA cycle. (More on this later). We wore suits on that day and IDs on lanyards so we looked official. It was this look that precipitated the most outrageous observations. People thought we were CIA agents. If you were a rational and educated person you might ask the question, why would CIA "Agents" be standing outside a bank all day? Which goes to prove some people have no sense of reality, watch too much television and jump to bizarre uninformed opinions with the minimum of information or rather misinformation.

Meanwhile back in the bank parking lot.

One of them replied he was there to see the Bank manager and named him.

I replied, "Yes, I just talked to him and he's inside."

"Good." The not so nervous man replied, "We're here to make a large deposit. We run a chain of laundromats." My new best friend explained.

"I'm in the wrong business. Gotta beat standing outside this bank in 90 degree weather."

"Yeah." He shot back finally breaking into a smile. "You can take that to the bank!"

What had started out as an unknown situation had evolved into a friendly encounter using the lightest of verbal judo and bodyguard presence. How simple was that? Yet I see such easy situations get blown out of proportion by over zealous security or bodyguards who were not paying attention in the first place then try to catch up on their OODA cycle and make the wrong connections. A seemingly casual and inquiring encounter can then turn ugly and lead to what? poor customer service? a bad relationship with your local security contact, in this place the bank manager, or losing a security contract because of heavy handedness?

The bank manager told me later how impressed two of his biggest clients were with the security at his bank. They used to feel unsafe coming into the bank with so much loose cash. Now they were singing the praises of the bank.

Of course all these bank security stories happened when banks were making money, could afford security and there was a serious attempt to protect bank employees and customers from armed takeovers of banks in specific high-risk locations.

OODA cycles - assessing situations quickly and effectively

In the military and law enforcement, in life and death situations, there are a series of processes that occur when assessing a stressful situation, quickly and efficiently. In a bodyguard school, they will teach you about OODA cycles, as this is a proven way to understand how we actually react to some rather nasty situations. You can apply this methodology to any situation. Any situation can be broken down into mental thought and physical action: Observe, Orient, Decide, Act. Or OODA for short.

First, we Observe what is going on, we Orient ourselves to the immediate environment, then we Decide what to do, then we do it, we Act. This is a decision making cycle, an OODA cycle. Fighter pilot and military strategist USAF Colonel John

Boyd devised this system of thinking and acting in time and motion, to win in fast paced aerial warfare.

If you have spent years practicing martial arts, you will have been told over and over again by your sensei that all the techniques, all the forms, all the movements you have repeated countless times will come automatically, when you get into a difficult situation that requires violent physical action. You would have proven this in competitions. But not so much in fighting in real life. Fighting on the street is fundamentally different from pretend fighting in the dojo.

In real life and in bodyguard situations, you have been able to react instantly to a physically stressful situation and come out the winner through speed, surprise, violence of action and maybe some luck! So although understanding OODA cycles is important, there are times, no pun intended, when you do not have the luxury of seconds or microseconds to think your actions through, for the situation demands an instant response.

Here is a commonplace example.

You are late for work, you want to catch a bus, rather than walk. You see where the bus is, behind you, (Observe) and the red light coming up. (Orient). You have enough time to run to the next stop if you cut across incoming traffic. You make up your mind to run across the road. (Decide). You run across the road, dodge traffic and catch the bus as it pulls up to the bus stop. (Act). These actions are all pretty spontaneous, it's not like you sat down to have a think about it, then acted. You went with the flow, so to speak.

Bodyguards use OODA cycles all the time, even if they do not realize they are using this way of processing challenges, threats and deliberating on actions to take.

Coming out of a restaurant after a late dinner you walk around the corner to where the car is parked. Your Protectee is behind you, you are doing a 5 second advance, keeping in front as you know what is behind you. You see a group of young men clustered around your Protectee's car. You count, there are 5 of them. (Observe). Definitely a "what is wrong with this picture" situation and you have little time to react or do "what if?" scenarios. You already know there are no cameras in the parking lot. The light is dim. There is no one else present in the parking lot and there is another exit on the other side of the lot. You cannot see anyone else in your quick 360 degree scan as you walk up to the group of men who have just noticed you. (Orient). You are positioned so the Protectee is directly behind you, about 3 steps behind. He has just seen the men and is about to mutter "what the fuck?" (Decide). In your left hand, you already have the small extra powerful flashlight that you shine right in their faces. (Act). You pull back your jacket and place your hand on your not so concealed firearm and say in a loud firm voice. "You guys are leaving right?" followed by "Over there." You point your gun hand in the direction of the other exit. They do not know if you have a gun in your hand or not. All they can see is that blinding flashlight. Not wanting to take any chances, but throwing away a few expletives to show how tough they are, they slowly back away. There is no damage to the car.

You keep the Protectee safely behind you, although he has seen enough to be rather uneasy and glad he had hired you. You then quickly get the Protectee into the car, and get out of the lot in the opposite direction to the departing young men. But you do not leave so quickly as to appear frightened. You look cool and you make it look casual, dare I say, mundane.

Back to the notion that you should document everything. It would be wise to write a report as to what happened and make a note regarding where to eat in the future. Perhaps this restaurant will not be on the list or you will park in another more open area.

Writing down brief notes also helps with report writing later. Bodyguards hate writing reports but sometimes this is what keeps a client happy or at least defines situations that can be analyzed at a later date. You also can cover your ass if something goes wrong. Even if you are not responsible, it was not your fault or you were not immediately present, chances are you will be blamed.

It's always the bodyguard's fault, is the unofficial mantra for many clients and Protectees who hire bodyguards and think of them as expendable (as in hire and fire) and way too expensive.

Learn from my mistake

It is the report you do not write that will cost you a contract. I know from experience. I had just finished providing a security detail for a multi million dollar jewelry consignment that was worn by a collection of female models in an exclusive fashion show in a new hotel. To make the situation even more chaotic, the Secret Service arrived as the President of the United States was due in a couple of hours.

My client told me that I would not be allowed to be with the models as they were female and would be undressing backstage. So I had to hire, at the last moment, a female bodyguard I had never worked with before and would never again. I had trusted my source who had said, don't worry she is good. She was so good, that when I called her, she could not answer her cell phone because it had been turned off. She had not paid her bill. Always a bad sign but it got worse. During the show, she had not kept track of the dizzying array of jewelry and costume changes the models had blitzed through backstage. At the end of the show after we had recounted the inventory, we were missing one piece. Not an expensive piece. It was only worth $8,000, one of the cheapest trinkets in the show, but still! The clients, the jewelry representatives who were supposed to be backstage keeping an eye on the changes and the goods, had been in the audience schmoozing and drinking cocktails. Now it was time to panic! A three martini panic! And whom did they blame? The bodyguard!

I made a few calls, found out which model last wore the cheap $8,000 trinket and where the model was. I drove with a very nervous employee of the jewelry store to her apartment. The model had been in such a hurry to leave the show she had forgotten about the piece on her wrist. Simple mistake. I took it back to the store and it was deposited into the safe with the rest of the multi-million jewels. No harm done. So I thought. Not taking my own advice, I did not write a report, where I should have outlined what had happened and all the weaknesses in the security protocols employed. Big mistake! Instead I went home and poured myself a whisky. Who got blamed for this? And rightly so as the bodyguard is responsible for everything, even if he isn't.

If I had written a full report, and sent this off the next morning, I might have kept the client.

So it pays to document everything.

Document what happens during your working hours, collect information related to your clients, alleged threats, security related events, equipment and training. Anything unusual happens? Write it down in your notebook. Take photos on your smart phone.

Information Junkie

Every operator I know is an information junkie. I collect everything I can about certain subjects: guns, knives, martial arts, herbs and spices, terrorists, extreme political movements, gangs, bodyguard schools and manuals, the list goes on and on. I am not joking about the spices. It is a sensible idea to collect recipes, especially quick nutritious meals that can be made in minutes. My office is full of folders, ring binders, filing cabinets and books stuffed with information I might need, have needed or just wanted to have for the hell of it. What I do not have in my office I have stored in digital format and backed up and backed up again.

Then there are always the private and public and not so public databases I can access for my investigations and bodyguard work. You can never know enough, never be too prepared or have enough information stored away for possible future use.

This goes back to my training for school track races. I could never be too prepared, too well trained. I never over trained. I was always properly rested and mentally ready to compete but there was that nightmare competitive athletes must have at some time in their career. I would dream I was at the start line and I was not ready. I had not trained enough. I was not at my peak. I was not physically or mentally prepared. This has carried over to my professional life and like a healthy dose of paranoia; it has kept me on my edge, alert and alive.

Document everything, for you can never have enough information.

Which leads me to compare bodyguards with investigators because there are many crossover skills and matching qualities and habits.

Chapter Seven

Good investigators make good bodyguards

For over a hundred years the United States Secret Service knew that good investigators made good Presidential bodyguards. All the skills to effect arrests and aid in the investigation of counterfeit money and currency fraud, protecting the Nation's money, could be used in protecting the President of the United States and high profile Government leaders.

These skill sets make for good investigators and good bodyguards.

The Seven Common Skill Sets between Bodyguards and Investigators

1. Surveillance and Counter Surveillance
2. The Art of the Field Interview, Micro Encounters and Extended Interviews and Interrogations
3. Decision Making
4. Understanding the Power of Intuition
5. Sources and Methods
6. Report Writing
7. Openness

1. Surveillance and Counter Surveillance

A skilled bodyguard knows whether he is being watched. This means having a sense of when, where, how and by whom you are under surveillance. It includes the ability to sense if any technical equipment is being used.

A lifetime of gawking at female bodies, or for women, checking out male bodies, provides the foundation for body language reading skills. Such youthful activities can translate into a mature evaluation of people in public and private places. How people react to each other and their environment.

Try an experiment next time you are driving, stare at the person in the car adjacent to you, in the next lane. See how long it takes for him to notice you are staring at him. Some people are aware immediately of you staring; others can take longer to pick up on you. Most people do notice. Does he freak out right away and accelerate? He can sense you are staring at him and it is unnerving. It's an aggressive act or at best antisocial, unless you are trying to get a date, highly unlikely in two different cars. My Editor wants me to take this staring into other cars while driving example out of the book and substitute staring at someone in a café or another public place where we are stationary, so there will be no accidents and therefore no liability. Where is the fun in that? We came to a compromise. Try staring at someone at a traffic light and see how uneasy he becomes. I did not tell my Editor that in South Florida, this alone could get you shot.

When you are conducting surveillance on someone, you do not stare at the target. It is best to observe him obliquely, to use mirrors, glass, windows, any trick in the book, but do not stare directly. Even long range surveillance can be picked up by someone who is intuitively connected to such actions. It is best to look at your target only occasionally. Even when following him, you do not stare at his neck or other body parts. Some people can pick this up, whether trained in counter surveillance or just naturally intuitive enough to sense that someone is looking at and perhaps following.

The person being targeted might be expecting surveillance. He might have experience in counter surveillance or have sound instincts about who could be looking at him. He could be paranoid or vigilant because of what he is doing or what he has been told. So it is best not to underestimate the state of mind of the target.

And do not take your surveillance cues from film or TV, where the actor continually stares at his target. It does not work that way. You have already done this in a bar, when you have stared at someone attractive and hoped that person would pick up on your staring and that person looks back at you. If she did, I do not want to know what happened next.

Whether you define this as an instinct or an acquired skill or a combination of both, you can only really hone these skills with thousands of hours of surveillance. We have all paid our dues by performing 12-hour shifts watching a door or a car or a building. These long hours of watching pay off, because you build up a sensory catalog of situations, experiences and locations whereby you can quickly assess what can happen. Call it streetwise sense or developed intuition but these skills are as vital for a bodyguard as they are for an investigator.

Having acquired such a catalog of experiences, you can look at a situation and quickly assess what is wrong with this picture?

Nothing beats the discipline of extended periods of surveillance, to observe, record and report back regarding a specific objective. Whether it be sitting in a tinted windowed car for 14 hours in a crime ridden neighborhood to record a specific person or spending 72 hours in a self dug hole in enemy territory, the experience is invaluable when it comes to protecting your client.

When you have successfully completed these hours of surveillance, you will be able to do the opposite, counter surveillance. You will know what to look for and what to sense, when someone is watching you. There are counter surveillance drills you can practice that a good bodyguard school will teach you and demonstrate.

Take for example when you arrive at your Protectee's house. Do you always arrive using the same route? Do you drive around the neighborhood and notice what is and is not out of place? Do you note other cars, vans, blacked out windows of vehicles you have not seen before?

The same counter surveillance mindset applies to where you live and how you approach and leave your house. How do you know someone is not following you? Do you alter your routes, double back or drive an unusual way to check up on your house and the neighborhood? Do you naturally scan the street when you walk out of your front door. I do not mean in an obvious way but in a casual looking manner so you can recall later who was where and what cars were parked nearby, including anything out of the ordinary? These become natural reactions when you are a bodyguard, part of your tactical mindset. The same goes for when you walk into a room or a new space, always checking out who is where, the location of the exits, what is going on in the room, any threats or unknowns that need to be noted or addressed. You are not doing any of these actions in an obvious B movie manner. It all appears very casual, relaxed, even unplanned.

Routines and repeated everyday occurrences take on a new meaning when you sense someone might be watching you or your Protectee. Do you always take the same routes at the same times? Are your travel schedules predictable?

Bodyguard schools study the history of assassinations. Be sure to study the history of dictators who survived or avoided assassination. There are lessons to be learned from how these long reigning dictators survived. Predictability or lack thereof is a common thread.

Fidel Castro, Yasser Arafat, Adolph Hitler and Joseph Stalin were all paranoid about being murdered. What special skills and techniques did they use to avoid being killed by their many enemies? They altered their routines and schedules continually, if they had any, changed travel plans at the last minute, slept in different locations, changed transportation unpredictably and did everything possible to outwit determined and watchful assassins. They also had a large contingent of bodyguards and a massive intelligence apparatus to protect them. Of the four dictators mentioned, Arafat lasted longer than he deserved, Castro as of this writing, is still alive. You will probably not go to such lengths to protect your client, but it pays to be aware of the immense amount of counter surveillance strategies some of the world's most despised and evil leaders have used to protect themselves.

2. The Art of the Field interview, Micro Encounters and Extended Interviews and Interrogations

Field Interviews

Anyone who has visited Israel can attest to how proficient Israeli security people are with their field interviews. I use the term loosely to mean any verbal or social interaction with anyone in a public or private space.

Israeli security methods emphasize the human factor in all situations.

Compare checking in at El Al at Ben Gurion Airport to checking in at an American airport. What a difference! And a terrible testament to how ineffective American security is in understanding very basic safety procedures. One of our first inner circles of protection is when passengers enter the terminal, check in their luggage and receive their boarding passes. Many American airlines, post 9/11, take pride in the fact that you do not have to interact with a human to check in. You can check your luggage and get a boarding pass by pressing a few icons on a computer screen. Your bags will be screened for explosives and prohibited items. Technology will make you safe. But no one has talked to you, or interviewed you, and asked about your destination, your baggage, how you are feeling. Your State or Federal ID card will be checked a few times against the name on the boarding pass, as if this is a way to spot terrorists. The security guard checking your name might not be able to speak or read English. And security is not allowed to profile; hence 80-year-old ladies from Wisconsin or retired

Homicide detectives from Miami are randomly checked for explosives and weapons.

One security guard at LAX thought I was the best selling writer Daniel Silva, whose visage was on the back cover of a book I held, Silva's latest hardcover adventure of Gabriel Allon, an Israeli assassin slash art restorer.

"That is you? Yes? Very handsome." She uttered in her best English. I showed her my Florida Drivers License with a photograph of the real me on it. To prove I was not Daniel Silva. There was no negative reaction from her. Yes, I was flattered she mistook me for someone who can write better and sells far more books, but really? If that security guard made a mistake with my identity, then how safe are we? A quick aside here, Daniel Silva's books are chock full of micro encounters, surveillance and counter surveillance episodes and the exploits of various bodyguards. Not to mention the talented Mr. Gabriel Allon and his skills. The novels are well worth reading.

At any El Al counter, anywhere in the world, the counter personnel are specially trained. They rely on the human factor not some multi-million dollar machine or a bar reading device. Yes, the latest technology is good, but nothing surpasses a well-trained and experienced interviewer. Before you check in, you are asked a few questions: Did you pack your own luggage? Did you always have it in your possession? Did anyone give you anything to take with you? A few more questions are thrown in too. Or they might ask you just two questions: How are you? And where are you going today?

The person behind the counter casually asks questions, but he is highly trained and is looking for anything unusual, any red flags. Out of this conversation, a look at your passport and its contents and the way you answer the questions, he will decide whether or not to let you go on to the next checkpoint or whether to pass you onto a higher level of screening from a more experienced interviewer who might just talk to you at the counter or draw you aside for more questions.

There has been no magical technology in the screening process so far, no state of the art scanning devices, just simple field interview techniques. The human factor is the secret here. It is so secret, that many in the U.S. Government security have never heard of it. The emphasis on the human factor is sorely lacking in U.S. airports, yet it is one of the first defenses we should implement for passenger screening.

Israel pioneers in high technology detection devices and there is only one major International airport. But they place human interaction first in a security approach consisting of many layers, from outside the airport where you car is surveilled to when your luggage is scanned

My wife and I were walking up to the Synagogue in Auckland, New Zealand. The Israeli guard outside, stood on the pavement, in a dominant position where he could talk to someone and at the same time keep a look out up and down the street for any pedestrians or cars. He made a note of our position as we walked up the hill. He saw us from a distance and when we approached he greeted us and asked us where we were from. We were going to Friday night services. We answered his questions, joked with him and we were let inside but afterwards we agreed that he had really screened us, and the way he had executed this field interview was impressive. I felt like I had been given a quick lie detector test, he was that thorough. All the security guard had done was some outer perimeter surveillance of us advancing to his position. He had time to assess who we were, our body language, our dress, what we were carrying. Then, for his field interview, he engaged us in conversation. He surmised we were attending Shabbat services at the Synagogue. I was impressed, as this was one more example of Israeli training and the triumph of the human factor. The entire process was completed without anyone getting bent out of shape or annoyed. The security screening was a pleasant conversation, spiced up a little, Israeli style.

I have seen the same field interview techniques used in Tel Aviv in the 90's. We were on a tour of recent terrorist attacks and we were outside the Dolphinarium Discotheque at a memorial. The memorial was for the 21 teenagers who were killed by a Hamas suicide bomber, and the 100's who were injured.

This was during the second intifada. There was an Arab man on a bicycle who was following us from a not so discreet distance and the two bodyguards assigned to our group wandered over to talk to him. Just a casual and non-threatening conversation in Arabic. Were they conducting a field interview? Of course, as they were on either side of the Arab on a bicycle, and kept a 360 degree view of everything around them.

The actual tourist group was unaware of the exchange and the dynamics and perhaps other players involved in the spontaneous field interview. This can lead to many reflections as to how security is played out in a civilized society. A large group of Americans are involved in an intense and emotional memorial ceremony for innocent young people who were killed by a terrorist. Yet a few feet away, security personnel are conducting a field interview and at the same time are establishing a secure perimeter, all while not attracting any attention, as if it was the most natural thing in the world.

Field interviews can be extremely short, almost like speed dating. If you do not ask what is going on, who are you, what are you doing here? How are you going to find out what is going on in your immediate environment?

Investigators like criminals, have a vested interest in perfecting their interview skills.

The Predator Interview

A human predator will select his next victim in a manner that criminal behavioral analysts like to identify as the interview process. This can be as fleeting as a glance at the potential victim. Then there is an evaluation of how the victim walks, how he carries himself and his body language. Some predators can intuitively pick out a victim, someone who is tailored to their criminal needs.

I interviewed a young predator in jail, who described to me in chilling detail, how he had selected an older female shopping for groceries, as his victim. He had observed her at the checkout and how she had carried her purse, how much money she had with her and her jewelry. She was unaware of her surroundings. She never looked around.

He explained how he had followed her home before robbing her at her doorstep. The victim was completely unaware of what had been happening around her and that she was a selected target. The attack did not just happen out of the blue but was preceded by target selection, surveillance, counter surveillance (were any police nearby?) and then a fast violent robbery of a victim who had no awareness of her predator's plan for her.

How many times have you watched a loved one walk to her car, never looking around or scanning the immediate area, then get into the car but leave the car door open as she fiddles with whatever she is fiddling with inside? And when she finally closes the driver's door, she spends another minute or two adjusting her hair and makeup with the door unlocked? Situational awareness does not mean you have to be always scanning your environment or living in fear or running from one locked space to another. It means just being conscious of what is happening around you. You do not have to be paranoid, you just have to be aware and exercise caution.

Micro Encounters

Micro encounters can be called fleeting interviews with little or no verbal communication; a quick body scan, a nod of the head, as two human beings pass each other. Such micro encounters are not to be underestimated in sizing up threats, opportunities or some other social endeavor. Another example would be a type of flirting, it is not a full scale field interview, more of a look, a smile, a quick word and walk on. I know a lot of bodyguards are big flirts. We like the ladies and we like to interact with them in open social and non threatening ways. It is a behavior we learned when we were much younger and have honed, or suppressed, depending on whom we are living with now.

A retired police officer, Paul Lupien, who founded the Miami Beach police department's Citizen Police Academy, was the master of the micro encounter. He taught through example how important it was to effect these small social exchanges that happen throughout the day and what lasting impressions they have on people. A good community oriented Law Enforcement officer can promote and develop profound connections with the local people he or she interacts with, by being professionally courteous. Paul taught that just saying hello, looking at someone in the eye, perhaps engaging in small talk, or asking a concerned question or two, forges alliances within a neighborhood. Community Policing is built on these micro encounters, that can develop into more sustained relationships. Growling and sneering at people does not make for a good connection with people you need to communicate with, whether you are in uniform or in plain clothes.

Bodyguards need to be open to social interactions around them, not that they have to be party animals but they cannot afford to be closed off and aloof from their environment. That said, bodyguards reflect the personality of their Protectee. If their Protectee is aloof, removed from everyone and does not engage in any social interaction, perhaps the bodyguard has to match such behavior.

There are times when we have to be friendly and talkative, then there are times and situations where we have to be aloof and unapproachable. In a sense, a bodyguard is a verbal ninja, where he knows how to physically and verbally communicate with strangers in unusual situations and get the strangers to do what he wants them to do as if the bodyguard was not there in the first place.

We all have our own style, our own manner of doing our job. As long as the Protectee is happy and we are not breaking any laws, we adapt our personal style to the current situation to get the desired results.

The same applies to being an investigator. I cannot repeat enough how many times I have hung around someplace and tried to talk to more people, just investing a few more minutes in a situation where nothing seemed to be happening and then someone has come up to me or I have discovered a new lead or witness. All because I did not leave as soon as I thought I had finished. I know there are times when you really want to get out of a certain place. The presence of vermin? A terrible smell? Unpleasant persons who look armed, lurking nearby and looking at you like a future victim? In cases like this, you want to be the person who is in the right place at the right time, rather than the opposite.

The Way of the Bodyguard is full of micro encounters and casual field interviews. There is no room for tough guys glaring at unknown persons or threats, as you will see what happens in the Chapter "Bodyguards in Film," a great example of what goes wrong when you do not conduct those seemingly trivial field interviews.

Extended interviews and interrogation techniques are also invaluable for both bodyguards and investigators. You will learn in bodyguard school about threat assessments and how to evaluate an entire spectrum of risk management options. But being able to read people in a variety of social situations quickly and accurately is a skill that bodyguards and investigators need.

3. Decision Making

Bodyguards, like investigators have to make quick decisions. That is why being aware of OODA cycles and how we make decisions is vital. This type of analysis and training is emphasized in many police departments and it is important to understand how we act in stressful situations. Decision making skills can be seen as part of leadership abilities: how to manage time, projects, people and stress. A good bodyguard school will cover this in detail.

In the blink of an eye

"Blink, the Power of Thinking Without Thinking" by Malcolm Gladwell is an excellent source of examples for how the mind works, especially for bodyguards. The chapter "Seven Seconds in the Bronx" sums up our challenges in terms of decision making in time and space. The synopsis of what happened in "Three Fatal Mistakes" is more poignant because the instructor who gave the lesson in "If you don't want to give up your life for your client then you can get your money back now" was the same firearms instructor who investigated the NYPD shooting. The bodyguard world is small.

Making an informed decision is different from acting intuitively. Sometimes you do not have the luxury of choices. Unless your choice is fight or run!

To use your instincts, you have to understand your intuition.

4. Understanding the Power of Intuition

Intuition, Instincts and Protection

When you observe, there is a part of your mind and body that absorbs other information. Have you relived an intense experience with a mixture of wonder and dread because you recognized certain signals and signs that made you change your behavior and avoid either an accident or a deliberate act of violence?

Knowing when to act before you have to act

Bodyguards and investigators have many stories about how they reacted to a bad situation before it actually happened, saving themselves and their associates. The explanation is that they felt something or they knew by instinct that something bad was about to happen and they took appropriate action. Whether it be the hairs on the back of their neck or a general feeling of unease, they had the instincts to change their behavior before something adverse happened. These instincts can be honed and developed through experience and training. I call it acting before you have to react, because action is faster than reaction.

The flip side to this sort of reaction is being able to respond intuitively and correctly. A mere beat can be the difference between a colossal screw up and a successful resolution to a stressful and fast moving situation. Of course in the real world you usually do not have a beat or even half a second to react correctly. If you can read the attacker's pre-indicators to an attack, the visual and verbal cues he is giving you, then you might be able to prevent the attack.

Gavin De Becker in his must read book "The Gift of Fear" describes this power of listening to and understanding your intuition. The root of the word intuition is "tuere," De Becker explains, which means to guard, to protect. Just like the Hebrew, "shomer."

There is a sixth sense we are born with, some of us have it more than others and some of us have developed it more, usually out of necessity. That is why I like working with former street cops who are now bodyguards, they can quickly read situations. They can call it before it happens.

I have broken down these instincts into five broad areas, which in turn answers the five main questions about human actions: When did it happen? Who made it happen? Where did it happen? Why did it happen? What made it happen?

The Five Instincts

The five questions are exactly what an investigator or bodyguard would ask about a particular event. The concept is that bodyguards can prevent or change events, before they happen, using these five instincts.

The Instinct of Timing:

The ability to time actions, knowing how to act and when. When will it happen?

The Instinct of Presence:

The use of bodyguard presence, how to use your physical and mental presence to change people's behavior or at least command the space around you. Who are you to use such a presence? Who will make it happen?

The Instinct of Experience in Spaces:

The practical knowledge of how to operate in open and closed spaces, and change, predict and influence other people's behavior in such specific spaces. Where will it happen?

The Instinct of Subtlety and Finesse:

The ability to work with subtlety and finesse despite lack of resources, lack of time and local knowledge. Why will it happen?

The Instinct of Understanding and Predicting Human Behavior:

The ability to somehow comprehend what another human being will do under certain circumstances. What will make it happen? Or if you are behind the OODA loop: what happened?

The linked concepts of intuition and instinct are worthy of much study, that is why most bodyguard schools recommend Gavin DeBecker's writing and why "The Gift of Fear" is so respected.

A Bodyguard's Instinct of Timing

As in comedy, timing is everything when it comes to being a bodyguard or an investigator. Being in the right place, doing the right thing with the right people requires planning, experience, a lot of skill and good instincts.

Knowing when to act, when to not act, when to anticipate the actions of others and their reactions, when to speak and when not to speak, where to stand, how to look, when to fight, when to protect, when to retreat into the shadows, when to evacuate the Protectee, it's all in the timing. This is simplistic, but it is a way of understanding time and space as in when will it happen for the bodyguard and when did it happen for the investigator.

The Investigator's and Bodyguard's Instinct of Presence

Presence might not appear an intuitive skill but understanding when to show or project your presence is. Again it is timing, knowing when to exert authority, when to blend in, when to create a high or low profile.

The Instinct of Experience in Spaces

Commanding the space means that you make sure there are no threats in the immediate area around the Protectee. Knowing how to operate in a low-key social situation, but observing and quietly controlling the immediate area is a skill not easily acquired.

There is a saying: "Close enough to protect, but not close enough to be introduced," that rings true in many social situations. Whether it be working with high profile celebrity clients to low key and tightly structured corporate executives.

The Instinct of Subtlety and Finesse

Working with subtlety is the ability to finesse a situation and either defuse it or turn it to your advantage, bearing in mind that you do not want to unduly scare or embarrass the Protectee. Or it can mean getting the right person to talk to you as an investigator.

The Instinct of Understanding and Predicting Human Behavior

The investigator asks what happened? The bodyguard will ask what will make it happen?

An investigator will interview witnesses, research databases and build up a profile on the person he is investigating, the incident that happened.

The bodyguard will study the potential threats, the potential targets and suspects and build a profile on the persons, the places and the events he is investigating to ensure nothing bad happens.

These skills where instinct is utilized, need to be continually improved upon; nothing beats practice and training, no matter how experienced you are. You have to be open to allow your instincts to work. To have an open mind, is part of the Way. But first there are sources and methods.

5. Sources and Methods

Bodyguards research clients, threats, advances, everything including the weather. Investigators dig up dirt, interview people of interest, document facts, collect verifiable information and then they dig up more dirt.

Both use sources and methods.

One of my favorite phrases is "Sources and Methods." Whether you are a first class intelligence officer, an elite bodyguard, a homicide detective, a patrolman, or an investigative journalist, you will have your sources and your methods.

You will want to constantly build up and develop your sources, be they human or electronic and you want to refine and acquire more methods to aid in your investigations or your bodyguard work.

When intelligence agencies share information they strip the information of their sources and methods, so as not to give away how they acquired it, whom they got it from and where they got it. The raw data is refined to a recognizable product that can be shared with other agencies without giving away how they acquired the product or from whom.

Law Enforcement Sources

Anything and anyone can be a source, not just the search engine of the moment or your buddy in local law enforcement.

In the "olden days," it was possible for a friendly LEO to share information with his non-police contact. Now everything bit and byte of computer information is sourced, cross-referenced and archived. Whoever is certified to access NCIC (the FBI's National Crime Information Center) and Local and State Law Enforcement databases is held accountable for what they access and see. When a LEO, who has restricted access to a government database like NCIC, pulls up a record, that transaction is stored for a long time. The LEO can be audited and the transaction questioned. Even pulling a license plate from a restricted database can get the LEO in trouble if it is not part of his or her investigation. So the days of your buddy in the police department sharing information is now severely limited. There are however private database conglomerates and resellers who provide almost the same amount of detail, barring of course actual Law Enforcement investigations. These open sources are not just typing in key words into a search engine but knowing specific web sites to visit to collect the required information. There are more and more open sources on the web everyday.

Open Sources

Bodyguards can access a wide array of information speedily to keep pace with any protective detail. Protectees change their minds, their routes, their destinations, and their plans. We ordinary mortals might dream of a vacation well in advance, book airline tickets at a discount and work out all sorts of bargain ways to make our hard earned money go further. A mega wealthy individual or celebrity with a private jet can indulge himself in ways we can only imagine. They, the super wealthy think and act differently. You will find this out the hard way, because even if you travel with them, you are not part of their magic circle, you are hired help and you are expendable.

There are sources and then there are Sources.

Your buddy in local Law Enforcement can no longer provide you with restricted printouts. Every Law Enforcement database query is sourced, accounted for and possibly audited. Besides, this is now illegal. But there are other human sources to be cultivated; whether it is a security director in an organization you will be working with or anyone who can provide you with critical, sensitive information to help with your advance or investigation.

Knowing when to keep your ears open and your mouth shut

Sometimes you cannot access local law enforcement sources. Arriving at a new city with a large contingent of the Saudi Royal family we were told by the commanding general not to tell the local police we were there. He did not want to have the

Family's presence announced. Not that you could keep so many people staying in so many hotels and spending so much money, cash money, a secret for long.

Three months later I am in a meeting at our Command Post (CP) with the local Special Agent in Charge (SAC) of the Secret Service who is coordinating the protective detail for a visiting Head of State. He turns to a lieutenant from the local police department and asks him if he knew we were here. The lieutenant says no. I have to apologize, saying it was the wish of our Protectee that I not have communication with any other authority. I felt uneasy that I made the lieutenant look bad or at least uninformed. My explanation sounded suitably conciliatory and diplomatic. We moved on to logistics. The SAC had already stated that the White House had told him to be nice to us, and not upset the Saudis.

They were impressed with our Command Post. The longer you stay on a detail in a hotel and the larger the detail, the more elaborate the Command Post gets. With all the equipment we had bought, begged and burrowed, it looked like a combination office and War Room.

The Command Post

With over 60 bodyguards, at least 40 drivers and seven locations, we had a large hotel room that had been converted into a Command Post. The beds and all furniture and wall decorations had been removed from the hotel room. We installed desks, chairs, notice boards, more notice boards, banks of computer monitors and rows of radio recharging equipment. Underneath the tables were stacks of Pelican cases with more gear.

We installed close circuit cameras on all entrances and exits, corridors and hotel elevators that we had secured on several closed floors at our main Headquarters hotel. The camera feeds were displayed in split screens on several monitors in the CP. We had two main desks staffed 24/7 by two CP personnel whose job was to run the Post. They monitored all radio and cellular traffic, the video feeds, the other monitors, the computers and kept a log of everybody's whereabouts so all activity on the floor and all entrances and exits were recorded. We also kept track of our Protectees. We had a dynamic database of contact information for everyone connected with our group. So there was a method to how we ran our CP. You can call it protocol, which sounds more important. But method is what method does.

Every bodyguard detail is different. You have to respect the wishes and the commands of the people in charge. Methods vary.

Other times it is common sense not to announce your presence at a hotel. I heard of one new graduate of a bodyguard school who boldly marched into the security director's office in a large Las Vegas hotel, to tell the director that he was bringing in some VIPs and that he was armed.

The security director promptly threw the new bodyguard out of his office and banned him from the hotel. No sources and no method!

There are ways to do particular things in certain places. Walking into a security director's office and making such an announcement cold, can only get him into trouble. If he had been introduced through a trusted source, then the meeting might have gone differently. His source would have informed him that mentioning firearms would get him kicked out of the hotel. Then there is the question of being armed. Security directors in Las Vegas hotels, as an example, do not like having unknown persons armed in their territory. He might be an ace shot, a local shooting club champion, whereas the armed security guard employed by the hotel only fires his weapon to qualify once a year. That is not the point.

When you step into a casino, you are in the security director's domain and he or she is in charge. You have to respect that. It helps if you do have any interaction with the security staff, that you have been introduced through the general manager who has impressed upon the security director to be nice to your detail, or another security director from another hotel who has vouched for you. For in Las Vegas, like any intense tourist destination, there are intricate and well-established professional networks of common interests. You are either in that network of trusted sources or you are an outsider.

Back to the security director of the hotel. If he does not know you are there, and there are thousands of people staying in his hotel and thousands more passing through each day, then he does not have to worry about you. You and your Protectee can stay low key. Unless of course your Protectee is a high roller or celebrity, then there is a different protocol. You would be interacting with different hotel personnel and your role would be defined differently. It depends on your sources.

There is a time to be low key and a time to be highly visible. Then there is a time when you do not want to hear what is being spoken about you.

Sources do not usually include eavesdropping as a bodyguard. For there are conversations we would rather not overhear:

"Oh he's just a new bodyguard we got. You'll like him, he's cute, a little old for my tastes but comes highly recommended. Sorry, forgot his name. He answers to anything."

Experienced investigators consciously develop sources from a wide array of human contacts in our culture. I make it a rule (that I break all the time – so it's a guideline not a hard fast rule) to have lunch with a source every week, schedule permitting. We share information, and help each other with problems we are having. Some people believe in the favor tree, you do a favor for someone and then later, you can call that person and ask for a favor in return. I think it is more positive and productive just to help people, your sources, when you can and not count how may apples you have left on the favor tree. As they say in the world of philanthropy, the more you give, the more you will get back. The more you help other people you come into contact with, the better you can develop more sources.

The phrase "how can I help you?" will win you more friends and sources than the question, "what can you do for me?"

Cultivating human contacts and learning to access new on line and off line sources can steer you in the right direction to win clients and solve problems but you still need "methods" to be able to solve these problems and build client confidence in your abilities. The method here is how you go about acquiring primary sources, actual eyewitnesses, how you cultivate human sources and how you conduct your business with integrity.

Methods include asking the hard questions related to when, where, whom, what, how and why? Verifiable evidence from primary sources and testimony that can be substantiated, are all part of the careful craft that investigators and body-guards use as part of their method.

6. Report Writing

It is the report you do not write that will get you into trouble. And this is worth repeating.

Writing clearly and concisely might appear a gift but it is a learnable skill that bodyguards need to master. There are many types, after action reports, advance schedules and threat assessments. Investigators take note; if you cannot speak clearly, how can you write properly? Both require that you express your ideas and actions in a coherent linear form that others can clearly understand.

Report writing ties in with acute observational and re-call skills acquired through thousands of hours of surveillance, counter surveillance and field interviews. Total recall, being able to describe in minute detail what has been observed, is a learned skill that can be honed by practice. Keep it simple and short and you will look good.

There are situations in bodyguard work where a well-written report submitted promptly will save your job, your contract, and your reputation. How will the Protectee or the client know what happened without being properly informed? What if someone else submitted a different version of the events that painted you in an unflattering or incriminating light? Who would the client believe? The bad report or the report not written.

Best to carry a notebook and make notes about events, or dictate into your smart phone, so the report you do have to write gets written.

7. Openness

My definition of openness is by definition wide open. And it is the opposite of being closed

Let me define what it is not with some examples.

I come across certain types of men all the time who say things like:

"I've been a detective for 27 years. There is nothing I haven't seen or heard. You can't teach me anything."

Then there is the investigator in the training session who states,

"I've heard this all before. My supervisor told me I have to attend. You gotta follow orders."

Or my favorite boast you will hear in a bodyguard school.

"There's nothing here I don't know, hell I could teach this myself, but I'm here for the contacts."

All such men have many negative traits in common, closed-mindedness being one of them.

They think they know everything, have seen everything, and are impervious to learning. They have closed minds.

Our technologically driven society is changing every day. I could say it is mutating at an alarming rate. But why be alarmed? We know there are changes happening in our environment, to our culture, to our technology all the time. Change, rapid change is constant.

It is natural for humans in their limited environments to only concern themselves with matters and technologies that directly affect them. And if they think they know everything, they are in a sense safer and feel more secure in their narrow world. Then it is more dangerous for you if you have to work with them in the real changing world.

The man who says he has seen everything, only means he has a narrow vision in processing his own limited experiences. He is not open.

A bodyguard who wakes up every morning and wonders what he will learn today and how he can be a better bodyguard, how he can improve as a human being, is following the Way. He is being open.

Our brains need to be open to new ideas, to absorb, to filter information, to learn and challenge our set beliefs and how we handle situations. That is why we love training. We are never too old to train. We are never too old to learn and we are never too old to question everything.

Pablo Casals, one of the greatest cellists, was asked why at age 93 he was still practicing three hours a day. He replied that he was starting to see some improvement.

Every skill we have is perishable. Yes, muscle memory from long term training, plays a large part in being able to execute gross motor skills in extreme situations but you still have to train, to practice. All physical skills are by definition perishable. We lose speed, agility, skills and strength over time but we have to be open to new ideas, new ways of doing things.

The Mixed Martial Arts Paradigm

When Mixed Martial Arts fighting first began in arenas, there was intense debate over which style was the best.

Experts made predictions that Gracie Jui Jitsu was superior to other styles because of all the winners that came out of this discipline, this way of training.

Then a Tae Kwon Do black belt won. No Karate black belts won any fights I watched. What was going on here? There is a saying:

It is not the arrow, it's the Indian.

We discovered that we were looking at the fighting style not the fighter.

Fighting is not about the fighting style, it's about the fighter.

Bruce Lee used to say your style of fighting should be that you have no style.

Successful fighters were open to new ways of training. No longer were they training like old school boxers or bodybuilders with weights. New ways, which essentially were very, very old school, were employed to achieve maximum physical fitness conducive to three five minute bouts in the Octagon. If you have ever fought, you will know that after about 30 seconds, or less, you have run out of oxygen and energy, unless you are highly trained for such intense physical work. 30 seconds can be a long time, in a fight. I am not talking about a street fight between two drunks who cannot fight and do not want to hurt each other, I am talking about serious bodily harm fighting.

In films, fights go on forever. They have to, it is assumed, to make them more realistic and dramatic. In real life fights are over in a few seconds and there is a body on the floor, or both bodies on the floor. Fights do not go on for minutes. Fighters run out of oxygen and energy.

Fighters began to mix up different disciplines and skill sets to win fights in the ring. There were some safety rule changes as well, but grappling, punching, kicking, wrestling, jiu-jitsu and other techniques and styles were mixed up for an open and personal fighting style that reflected the fighter's mental and physical make up.

The Mixed Martial Arts fighting phenomenon changed our attitudes towards the martial arts and fighting and reinforced new ways of fighting. Hand to hand combat was seen for what it was, chaotic violence. New ways of training and fighting were validated in the ring. Even if some of these fighting and training ideas were centuries old, from Russia and further East.

Learning Immune Impairment Syndrome ©

Back to the bodyguard or investigator who is stuck in his old way of seeing his limited world, and refuses to challenge himself, his ideas, his techniques, his skill sets.

I call this Learning Immune Impairment Syndrome (L.I.I.S.) ©; the ability of some men to be close-minded and set in their ways, unable to conceive they are wrong or that they should re-evaluate their initial conclusions or actions. Avoid these people.

In the bodyguard world, everyone's an expert

To follow the Way of the Bodyguard you have to be open, and be able to question established ways of seeing the world.

When you are dealing with men with guns, egos and reputations to guard, and money to be made; everyone is an expert.

One of the first tasks you must undertake to follow the Way of the Bodyguard is to lose your ego.

Chapter Eight

Bodyguards and Samurai

To lose your ego is the ultimate Zen act

There was a mythical time when a dedicated samurai would get up every morning knowing that that particular day could be the last day of his life. He had to be prepared for death at any moment and accept his fate willingly. He took extraordinary preparations for his end, including shaving, washing and combing his hair. In one sense, he had an open mind because he was prepared to die, at any time. At one stage in the Feudal wars, samurai would spray perfume on their heads, so if they were beheaded and their helmets fell off, their attacker would have the appropriate perfect olfactory experience while observing the severed head. With decapitation comes a tremendous amount of arterial blood and a smell difficult to forget. This perfect olfactory experience is a myth.

We have been led to believe these myths in the West. American writers repeated these descriptions, depicting samurai in romantic and heroic warrior roles.

Allied heroes who survived World War Two and who encountered such samurai spirit up close and personal had a different interpretation. My father met samurai warriors in the jungles of Burma. He had a large collection of officer swords that he had picked up in the morning from the surrounding wasteland of artillery trenches and barbed wire, after a night of furious charges across fields of machine gun crossfire and hailstorms of grenades. These swords reminded him of his first day in Burma when a Japanese plane dropped color photographs of English prisoners of war. The emaciated men were half naked, kneeling, their hands tied behind their backs. The prisoners were in various stages of being beheaded with samurai swords.

Times have changed. We do not compose death haiku today.

But there are still those in our profession who compare present day bodyguards to samurai. Samurai no longer live in a brutal highly regimented feudal society that saw the blossoming of Bushido, the way of the samurai in Japan from the Tokugawa Shogunate in the early 1600's through to the opening of the Japan to the West by Admiral Perry in 1854-56.

Samurai, or at least the mythical and romanticized warriors we read about today, possess many traits that bodyguards should have: honor, fierce courage, strong instincts, a profound sense of justice, an enormous array of technical weapons expertise and fighting skills, and complete loyalty to their master, their daimyo, their Lord.

We should not overly romanticize samurai as a class. Many were hired killers, bullies and assassins for ambitious and brutal rulers. Rather, we should look to the role of Miyamoto Musashi and other revered samurai and Zen masters as examples we can learn from.

Musashi and the Way

Bodyguards should study Musashi's writings closely and meditate on how he can guide and inspire us. See the Way of the Bodyguard Reading List for samurai and Zen books, in particular William Scott Wilson's translations of Miyamoto Musashi's The Book of Five Rings and Takuan Soho's The Unfettered Mind, as well as the new graphic novel from Musashi's The Book of Five Rings adapted by Sean Michael Wilson. To bring Musashi into perspective, I strongly recommend Eiji Yoshikawa's excellent fictional saga called "Musashi."

Modern Day Reality

Here are some of the qualities we look for in a modern day bodyguard.

The essential qualities I look for in a bodyguard are as follows (and I use "he" when I mean he or she. I have worked with some awesome female bodyguards.)

Does he know himself? Is he at peace with who he is? He can be hungry, have an offbeat sense of humor, but he still has to have that discernable quality I call inner peace. Someone who won't get ruffled when the *drek* (that's Yiddish for shit) hits the fan. Someone who has nothing to prove, because he's proved himself many times and has no need to put his team and his Protectee in danger to show how tough he is.

Does he have good instincts? Can you trust his intuition that is enhanced by experience? Is he more than streetwise, is he actually able to sense when things are about to go wrong and take appropriate action?

Is he in good physical condition, not necessarily huge and muscular, but can he survive a long grueling day with no breaks, intense demands and still exhibit grace and calm under pressure?

Can he laugh at himself? Does he have a sense of humor? A highly developed sense of humor is an indication of intelligence. If he has no humor he is probably as dumb as a doorknob, even if he is built like a door!

Does he have a physical presence? You do not have to be 6 foot 3 inches and 235 pounds of hard muscle with close-cropped hair to look intimidating. It sure helps but a smaller, lighter man can still project a professional and no-nonsense presence. There should be a quality in his eyes and an authority in the way he holds himself that projects a firm measure of intelligent protection.

Of course there are essential skills and the required experience needed for such a demanding and technical job but these can be learned. The above qualities are innate, they cannot be learned, only honed.

Then there is the quest for perfection and endless training. Can he keep on training, keep on trying to improve himself, even after weeks of 12 and 16 hour shifts? Training is endless, be it with firearms, edged weapons, hand-to-hand or other skills, like languages, security driving or cooking. Who is going to be hired for the next security detail? The man with the iron fists or the man who can cook up a meal for everyone in the Command Post and make superb coffee?

Chapter Nine

Today is the Last Day of Your Life.

My favorite chapter title illustrates how unpredictable and vicarious our profession is.

Death awaits bodyguards

Anyone in the military, law enforcement, corrections and the protection business should understand how swiftly you can go from living to dead.

I do not offer these examples to illustrate what they did wrong. I am not second guessing anyone here. We do not need any more armchair bodyguards.

All woke up on the last day of their life thinking that nothing much was going to happen, that today was going to be like any other day. They did not know today would be the last day of their lives.

Taking every day for granted is dangerous. Mediocrity is dangerous. Thinking that nothing can happen to me is dangerous. A complacent mindset is dangerous. I try to think what could go wrong on this job, what would I do, how can I prevent these bad things from happening? When nothing is happening, I do not take such quietness for granted. You cannot take anything for granted.

Here are four examples of the last day:

Two bodyguards were ordered to board a plane, not designed for nine people and luggage in excess of safe weight limits.

An older security guard thought he could out draw a gunman who already had a 9 mm pistol pointed at him.

For lack of a bodyguard, a high profile businessman with some questionable associates, is gunned down on a street in South Florida. He had considered hiring at least one bodyguard but thought it was too expensive.

A driver speeding too fast in a tunnel in Paris tries to outrun motorcyclists with cameras, only to crash and kill the two celebrity passengers and seriously injure the bodyguard.

I do not judge these people. They are dead. They cannot argue back. You only have to be unlucky once in this business, really unlucky. And their problems, their challenges are ours. Take the Type A personality who demands you do something, even though it is against your better judgment. What do you do? Defy your Protectee? And lose your job? We are expendable. They can hire someone else.

Example One

Sunday, August 25th, 2001, Bahamas.

Aaliyah wanted to get back to Miami. She was a rising actress and music star. Now we have virtually forgotten who she was. The scheduled charter was not at the airport. She demanded another plane. There was a Cessna 402-B present and a pilot was procured. The plane could safely carry eight people and a little luggage. They had nine and lots of luggage. Aaliyah couldn't wait. The two bodyguards had no time to check out the pilot, go over the log book, do their own pre flight check. The twin-engine plane, loaded, was at least 900 pounds overweight, the pilot had cocaine and alcohol in his system and the plane itself was not well maintained. Like most airplane disasters there was a confluence of factors that built up to and created a catastrophic effect. The plane fell out of the sky. All were killed. One of the bodyguards, Scott Gallin was right out of Central Casting for celebrity bodyguards. He was huge, solidly built with a strong presence but if you got to know him he was gentle and relaxed. He was the type of bodyguard who walked into a room and you would have said, yes, I want to work with him.

What do you do when your Protectee says we are going on this plane, even if your instinct and all your training screams "NO!" I said I am not second-guessing anyone and I am not because I would have gotten on that plane as well. Do you think I would want to be stranded without a job, without a plane ticket, in Marsh Harbor, in the Bahamas and have to hear from the record company the next day: "You did what? You'll never work for us again." No one wants to hear "You'll never work in this town again!" We all want to keep our jobs. Well, some of us do. In the real world, you do not have the luxury of second guessing your Protectee. If she says we are going, that's it. You have to go along with the plan and adapt.

There are lessons to be learned from this tragedy. Check out the pilot, if nothing else, he has a Pilot's log. The plane has its own maintenance logbook, the charter company has a history and if it doesn't look or feel right, try and convince the Protectee or the client or anyone to change plans. Good luck, because if you are stuck in that kind of situation you probably will be without cell service, without internet access and no one will be available to answer your questions.

What would be worse is if you did not get on the plane and you watched it fall out of the sky. You would still have to answer to some very angry record executives and family. You lost your Protectee and her entire entourage.

There is never a happy ending to such situations and again I am not second-guessing or paying anyone disrespect. I would have gotten on the plane. I have been in dramatic situations where the Protectee, the client, screams they are doing this when everything you know and feel screams NO! You should not do that! Nothing illegal, just unsafe and unwise. But you go ahead anyway because you do not want to lose your job, and nothing is going to change the Protectee's mind.

Example Two

I was witnessing an autopsy at the Miami Morgue at 1 Bob Hope Way in the Jackson Medical Center, Miami, when the assistant Medical Examiner came over to me and said let me show you this. You have already read this story but it is worth retelling here from another perspective.

The corpse looked huge, the stomach bloated, on the steel table. The chest cavity was opened up. She explained what had happened. "The bullet's shock wave burst the aorta then went through his spinal cord and out his back. He was dead before he hit the floor."

I added: "I read they dug the bullet out of the wall, a 9 mm full metal jacket, it didn't mushroom."

She nodded and continued: "Look what they did at ER, they opened up his chest, massaged his heart and gave him massive amounts of blood, but he was already gone." She pointed out the stitches, the handiwork of care and love that went into trying to save this poor security guard who was already beyond saving.

I told her I had a client I was protecting whose brother was the lead First Responder at the scene, a large jewelry store at the Village of Merrick Park in Coral Gables in December 2002. The EMS crew had tried diligently to save the security guard's life.

Just one bullet, a full metal jacket 9 mm. Experts debate what is the best caliber for one shot kills, but looking at the corpse, it did not matter. One bullet killed him, not a larger 45 S&W or a jacketed hollow point 9 mm.

In training, especially force-on-force training, we learn very quickly, sometimes the hard way, that reaction is slower then action. But we do learn, because we get up, endure the bruises and realize the sheer physics of the equation. Action always beats reaction.

If you have done any fighting, you have also learnt this. So the security guard was sitting on his stool and did not react to the group of young men who were walking up and down the mall outside the jewelry shop. There was video of the mall that clearly showed the young men were casing the place. When the lead robber came in with his 9 mm handgun drawn, officer Brito got off his seat and went to draw his own .38 special revolver.

A friend of mine, Eric Dybing, who ran a security company, wrote a letter to the local newspapers and called for the Brito bill making it mandatory that security guard companies supplied bulletproof vests to guards in high risk posts. He invested his money in what he believed in, because all his men in Bank Robbery suppression details wore bulletproof vests, even in 90-degree heat and 90% humidity. There are few things worse than standing in 90 degree heat and feeling sweat run down your back and legs and wishing you did not have to wear a bulletproof vest. I know because I have stood in sweat filled shoes wearing such a vest that gets heavier by the hour. But I have to remember that I would rather be uncomfortable standing, than lying on that slab.

Eric stresses that he in no way lays blame on the security company or on officer Brito. But some of the questions raised were:

1. Was the guard properly trained for this post?
2. Was the guard in a good tactical position?
3. Is the deployment of a single armed officer appropriate?
4. Why did the guard engage so many subjects?
5. Did the guard see all the subjects?
6. What were the post orders for the guard?
7. Why did the guard go for his gun when clearly outnumbered?
8. Why did the mall not have armed police officers?

He also asks if the officer was wearing a vest, would he be alive today? It is a good point and one to remember when you think, nah, I'll leave it home (or in my car) today.

The mall later switched to an on duty Coral Gables police presence, and the jewelry store had a Coral Gables off duty officer present when they were open. The same security precaution applied to the Miami Beach store on Lincoln Road. As one local cop told me, if they don't have an officer present, they get robbed. Well, it has happened several times, but please note, the off duty officers wear their vests.

How many times have you taken a high-risk detail and not worn a vest? There are very thin and cool vests available now. Yes, they can cost from $500 to $1,000, but have you ever seen an ER bill for even minor trauma?

What is your life worth? As well as a Level III A vest, I also have a Kevlar T shirt that has a drop in 8 x 10 inch pocket for a trauma pad. I can even hide a weapon or two under each arm in a special compartment. So I have no excuse not to wear protection.

Example Three

The High Roller Businessman who did not hire a bodyguard

Sometimes as a bodyguard you do not have a choice as to what to do. Just like the situation in Example 1, you do what the Protectee says and what your client demands. They do not teach you this in bodyguard school although it is a worthwhile scenario to game play: A wealthy long-term Protectee wants to engage in high-risk behavior. You object, but short of resigning on the spot you cannot change the situation or what is about to happen. If you go ahead, you go into extreme peril. If you resign and do not go with your client you are allowing him or her to advance into danger without you. The Secret Service might be able to say to the President of the U.S.A., "No. We are not doing this. It is too risky." But you, as a private hired bodyguard cannot say this without losing your job. And if the Protectee is harmed or killed while you have bowed out of the assignment or resigned? Where does that leave you? You should have been there to protect!

Then there is the situation where the person under threat decides not to hire a bodyguard. Even though he has received information that his life is in danger.

Gus Boulis, a controversial and suddenly very wealthy businessman, had called someone I knew who hired himself out as a bodyguard. The bodyguard had a reputation for high-risk jobs and the way he walked reflected the fact that he had broken many bones in his body from various adventures he had undertaken. I will call him John and provide a caveat that John attracted trouble. He no longer lives in South Florida but he had a searing intensity that could bring out the worst in people. John told me about the call a few weeks later when we were on another job together protecting a gypsy.

Perhaps Gus Boulis sensed this when he called John and asked him how much he would charge for some bodyguard work. He told John that there was little risk but he was wondering how much would John charge for riding around with him for a few days. John sensed there was more to the story. There almost always is and we know from experience that hard charging businessmen are reluctant to bare their fears or safety concerns to a stranger over the phone, no matter how professional the stranger, read bodyguard, is.

John quoted an hourly rate and a daily rate for a week that was reasonable for the time and considering the unknown risk. In hindsight, it was very reasonable. Gus Boulis objected to the price and hung up. Several days later, on February 6th, 2001, Gus Boulis was gunned down while driving alone in his BMW, on a street in Fort Lauderdale. He became rather belatedly a poster boy for what happens when you do not follow your instincts and dig into your wallet and pay a few thousand to someone to protect you, with their life.

I cannot speculate that if Gus Boulis had hired John that John would have avoided the ambush from allegedly two shooters in one car and the other car performing a blocking motion, but I do know John has been in some very violent situations and conducted himself rather well. I like to think John would have shot his way out of the situation and saved Gus Boulis, even if it meant taking a few bullets in the process.

Gus Boulis had an upcoming court date. By hiring a bodyguard, lets say John, he would have invested a few dollars in protecting his life. Looking back, you can see that spending a couple of thousand on protection is infinitely preferable to being gun downed. The hit men were not trained killers like Spetsnaz or Special Forces operators. They were gangsters who got lucky. Gus Boulis was not lucky.

Reference:
http://en.wikipedia.org/wiki/Konstantinos_%22Gus%22_Boulis

Example Four

Death of a Princess

The car accident deserves another look because the situation highlights how just one bodyguard cannot be in control of the entire situation. In an extremely visible protection detail, where there are many elements involved, including a remote Command Center giving orders and many players, there are times when the bodyguard's objections are ignored. Sound familiar? It should. If you have worked on large-scale celebrity bodyguard details, there are always competing views and interests, and your security concerns might not get the credence they deserve. No one listens to you.

The Final Official British Government Report still leaves some muttering conspiracy, including Princess Diana's alleged soon-to-be father in law.

Metropolitan Police Commissioner Lord Stevens released the long awaited and supposedly definitive 832 page report in December 2006. The Report's conclusion was that Princess Diana (aged 36) and Dodi Al Fayed (42) died when their Mercedes crashed in a tunnel shortly after midnight (00:25) 31st August, 1997. The driver was drunk and under the influence of prescription drugs (the alleged original blood tests revealed he was three times over the blood alcohol limit - for France!) and he was speeding, attempting to outrace pursuing photographers when he lost control.

Many personal protection specialists and security experts have written at length about this tragedy. Dodi's father hired a top investigator to conduct his own inquiry and a series of disturbing facts evolved from this independent inquiry but it is not the purview of this chapter to raise, dispute or concur with alternative theories as to what happened.

I want to make a point about who is really in control in high profile bodyguard jobs, the bodyguard or the well known and powerful figure or the Client, the Protectee or the Command Post? And do you tell your Princess to put on her seat belt? Especially when the driver and the bodyguard do not have their seat belts on? There was speculation that she could have been saved if she and Dodi Al-Fayed were wearing their seat belts.

Background to disaster

Several factors contributed to the tragedy. Like an airline disaster there is an accumulation of errors and events that result in the ultimate tragedy. Remove one or more of these events and the crash might not have occurred.

Princess Diana refused Scotland Yard's professional bodyguard service. The Princess used Dodi Al-Fayed's personal bodyguards. The Princess also did not utilize her own or Dodi's bodyguard driver. The Ritz's assistant chief, the chauffeur used by its celebrity guests, Henri Paul was hired. This fact was stressed by Rees-Jones's lawyer in the bodyguard's public defense. Lord Stevens' Report stated as had previous testimony, that Henri Paul the driver had a blood alcohol level of three times over the limit allowed in France, that he had been taking prescription drugs and he was driving at twice the speed limit when he lost control in the Alma tunnel.

The Driver - Security Risk

As bodyguards we have all been in situations where we have selected, trained and worked with elite bodyguards. We work as a discrete team and know what the other thinks, how he acts and so on. Then there are the drivers. Rarely do we get to select and train the drivers. Drivers always seem to be a weak link. We are assigned drivers by the client, or an outside source, or another person involved in the security detail, perhaps someone saving money or making money on the side.

Of course there are good drivers. Then there are bad drivers. And then there are drivers who drink. I do not work with bodyguards who drink on the job. That includes off the clock. If you are always on call, working long hours every day with no day off, then when can you drink? The answer is never. What if you are called up and asked to do something in the middle of the night? Ok there are some ex-Special Forces bodyguards who still drink after their shift and manage to be fully operational the next day but they are the exception and ultimately, over the years, this drinking catches up on them and shows in their face, their body, their attitude.

What happened in Paris

According to the final French report delivered by Judge Herve Stephan who presided over the most extensive investigation into a traffic accident in French history, the Ritz driver, Henri Paul, at the time of the crash, was three times over the legal alcohol limit. The English report by Lord Stevens reiterated this fact.

Who was in control?

Trevor Rees-Jones was not in control of the situation. As a bodyguard for a very high profile client, you hardly ever are in control. You are reacting to and adapting to situations that are thrown at you. He was aware of the plan to use a diversion at the Ritz Hotel. Henri Paul was called back as the driver. He was supposed to be off work. It appears that Rees-Jones had no say in whether Henri Paul was competent enough to drive. During their last fatal drive, Rees-Jones could not change the driver's speed or style of driving. Nor could he counter-mand any alleged instructions the Princess and Dodi gave to the driver. As quoted in the French Magistrates' final report (see below) - 'Trevor Rees-Jones even stated: "Dodi took an active part in security arrangements, he was the boss and in addition we did not know the programme in advance, only he knew the programme." '

When can you tell the client, the Protectee, what to do?

Apparently, if the Protectee is a Princess, in title or not, the answer is at best, not often. The Protectee is in charge and does not have to listen to security advice, nor supposedly heed any directives or orders. When dealing with strong minded clients, the failure of the Protectee to follow directions or take advice regarding their security can be challenging at best. This is a fact of life for bodyguards. We have to get used to this reality.

Reality versus Theory

No matter what bodyguard course you take or executive protection book you read, the fact of the matter is, if they have enough money to hire you, they can do what they like, including fire you, if you keep on being a nuisance with directives, commands, and orders. Remember, you are still only the bodyguard. Your job is to serve and protect them. You are staff, like the cook, the baker, the candlestick maker.

If you can influence their behavior, condition their responses and somehow change their strongly held and unsafe practices and views, you are doing a great service to them and yourself.

When things go wrong, you will be blamed. No one said it was easy.

References:

The Bodyguard's Story: Diana, the Crash, and the Sole Survivor by Trevor Rees-Jones, Moira Johnston

Princess Diana Final Crash Inquiry Report by Lord Stevens, 2006, Operation Paget.
http://en.wikipedia.org/wiki/Operation_Paget

Who is more at risk? Bodyguards or Cops?

Not a fair question as there are far more Law Enforcement officers in the U.S.A. than bodyguards. You only have to read the newspapers to see that police officers get killed almost daily in the U.S. OK so it's a big country with over 300 million population but seeing so many cops killed demonstrates that their job is as dangerous if not more so than a bodyguard's. Check out the web site policeone.com and the section named Officer Down. It is a sobering fact. We lose so many good officers.

Overseas is a different matter. Even in Paris, France. Take the death of Princess Diana.

Admittedly the bodyguard did not die, but it was close. He was saved by his passenger side air bag. His Protectees died.

Who's next?

Who's next? You? Type the words "bodyguard killed" in Google. You will come up with a long list of bodyguards killed in high-risk areas overseas. There are very few bodyguards killed in the U.S. Get the picture?

Think about it. Where do you want to work? What precautions are you going to take? Who do you want to work for? Would you risk losing your job to speak up on a critical issue?

There could be a lone gunman planning a violent action where you will be tomorrow. You could be present at that event. Are you ready?

Is tomorrow the last day of your life?

Which brings me to client selection. It is a fantasy that we actually pick clients. We usually accept any client we can. If they pay, we protect. But there are certain questions that need to be asked.

For one, is taking this new client worth the risk?

Chapter Ten

Client Selection is Natural Selection

If the Way of the Bodyguard centers around self knowledge and the quest for perfection, then it behooves the bodyguard to know his client. You have to understand whom you are protecting.

Whenever I get approached by a potential client, I like to check out who they really are. The internet provides a wealth of open source information especially if the new client is high profile. I run a background check on them as well from a private database that can tell me everything I need to know about them without getting subpoenas or court orders. What do they own? Where do they live? What do they do for a living? Is he married, single? A party boy? Does he have other interests? The list can get rather long. I do this discretely. But before I sign a contract with my new Protectee I want to know what I am getting into. There are some clients that are not worth the trouble. Then there are the clients who are doing something illegal and do not tell you.

The drug dealer client

"I only need you for an hour but I'll pay you for the four hour minimum."

That is a red flag. Who wants to have a client for only 4 hours. Yes, we need to make money but by the time you figure in traveling costs and the time it takes to check out this new client, is it worth the effort? We want long term clients.

There are variations but they go something like this. A businessman wants you to watch his back while he meets a new client. It will be in a public place; a bar, a parking lot, a hotel lobby. He says he will meet this new contact at a certain time, and he wants you nearby. "You don't have to be next to me but nearby. And look menacing. I don't want to introduce you but I want him to know you are there for me." Then he lays on the false flattery that seals the deal. "I know you're worth it but I'll pay the full four hour minimum. This will be over in under an hour." And then "I'll pay cash. So there's no sales tax right?"

The meeting is a drug deal. Do you really want to participate in this? Ignorance is not a defense, only a poor excuse for not exercising discretionary judgment.

The fighting client

I drove up to a very large MacMansion that looked more like a hotel than a real home to meet a money trader. He said over the phone that he liked to go out partying Friday and Saturday night. He had his own limousine and driver. I wondered what had happened to the other bodyguard he used. A long talk with the limo driver, while we were waiting for the Master of the Universe, filled in the blanks. The old bodyguard had been arrested for fighting. The Protectee liked to get drunk and pick fights knowing that his bodyguard would back him up and finish off the fight. Even with a big cash tip, this job was not worth the trouble. But just to be sure, I subbed this out to a trusted bodyguard. He reported back the next morning. It happened exactly as the limo driver had predicted. The bodyguard, a very tough Marine, said he would never work for that client again.

"This guy is crazy. He gets drunk and picks fights. I am lucky I am not in jail."

Next week I picked up the check and parted company with the fighting client.

The not quite honest client

There are clients who never tell you the entire story right away, because you do not need to know everything. But you do want to know everything. That is your job. They want your help but they do not want to tell you the full story, for many reasons. They are embarrassed. They do not want to divulge too much personal information to a complete stranger, a hired hand. They might not understand the full implications of their threat or situation where they find themselves needing a bodyguard. There is always something they hold back.

I had one client together with his wife who was anxious, if that is a better word than terrified, of some East Europeans who were trying to take over their business. How did I find this out? Several months later, the husband mentioned he had worked it out with the Armenians, and they were OK now. That was a relief. The Armenians are OK now. What! I never knew about the Armenians. How many were they and what was the dispute about? Was this a cue for me to say I would not be employed by them any more? He also told me he had just imported their third Belgian Malinois from the Czech Republic to guard their country house. And I thought I was protecting them from a stalker. Not the Armenians!

The fantasy client

The better known you are in the bodyguard business, the more lunatics and fantasists you attract. I would get calls from delusional women who thought they needed a bodyguard. For several months, I received calls from a young woman who said she had just signed a major recording contract and she needed me as her personal bodyguard to tour the country. It was a great fantasy I must admit but a quick call to the record label revealed no such contract.

Another time I got excited for a few hours for a young man who was traveling to Sierra Leone to pick up an older couple there to bring them back to the U.S. He said he had taken care of everything. He had an answer to every question I threw at him. Then I looked up his address on Google Earth and it was a small house in a working class neighborhood. The place did not look rich enough to support his fantasy plans. The caller was in turn being conned with a Nigerian Advance Fee scam. A check on his civil court filings showed he had almost made himself bankrupt over the last year from participating in the fantastic scheme he had become involved in. He had gotten deeper and deeper into debt. He was the victim. He would not admit this when I told what I thought had happened to him. He was in denial and could not face the reality of his situation. I did not send the highly trained bodyguard who was about to escort him first to Spain to pick up the money then onto Sierra Leone to pick up the couple.

The honest client

Then there are clients who are totally honest. He had been threatened by an ex-customer who lived a few blocks away in the same gated community. The client had a very clear under-standing of whom the threat was and how it had originated. We set up 12-hour shifts, with a bodyguard in his car, outside the client's house. This continued for a couple of weeks until the client went to court.

While standing with him outside court before the hearing, I managed to work out a deal with his adversary's attorney and we agreed on a compromise that avoided some substantial legal fees. On my advice he also sent a large box of Godiva choco-lates over to his adversary's house, who, because he lived in the same fancy neighborhood, would never have lived up to any sensible stay away order. The adversary did not lose face, he gained stature with his wife, and felt vindicated and happy. He had won, whatever that meant to him and his ego.

Winning by losing

My client's attorney was initially furious but knew this was the best solution to what could have become a meaningless and endless series of expensive legal maneuverings. The two did not become friends but they were no longer enemies. My client won by losing. Call it a Zen thing, but it worked. He saved a lot of money and a lot of anxiety over his family's safety that was his paramount concern.

Quick aside here: in our first long phone interview, late one Saturday night. My wife was furious, as we were in a restaurant, a rare treat for a bodyguard and his wife. The honest client stressed that he was more worried about his family's well being than winning some vague legal battle.

In our first face to face, I could see he was genuinely concerned for his family and would put them first before his pride or business practices or whatever motivates Type A personalities to always win. That job only lasted two weeks. But I did the right thing and saved the client a lot of heartache and anxiety over what was a simple solution to a simple problem. I also saved him a lot of money.

Chapter Eleven

Bodyguards in Film

There are several examples of Bodyguards in European and American film. Denzel Washington in "Man On Fire" is a prime example. But who hires a drunk? We find out in the movie. Real life does not imitate the movies. I have never heard of an American carrying a firearm in Mexico. It does not happen. Even the FBI cannot carry firearms in Mexico. It is against Mexican law. To see bodyguards in action for an extended period, you need to watch Brian De Palma's "Femme Fatale."

It is a great teaching tool. My instructions go like this.

"I am going to show you a few minutes of a film. Pay attention to the bodyguards. What do they do right? What do they do wrong? Take copious notes because we will go over this in detail." That's the set up.

Brian De Palma's "Femme Fatale" (2002)

Two bodyguards make nine classic mistakes

A news search for the term "bodyguard" on the internet reveals a series of unfortunate consequences for bodyguards:, being tried for murder, not stopping a client from being embarrassed in public or even worse, death by association. There is never any good news printed about bodyguards. You will never see the headline "Bodyguard ensures nothing happens." If you make the news, as a bodyguard, you are in trouble or you are already dead.

Bodyguards in film suffer similar fates. And the two tuxedo clad bodyguards in Brian De Palma's overlooked film noir provide wonderful examples of how easily things can go wrong.

The opening sequence to "Femme Fatale" entails an elaborately choreographed diamond heist at the 2001 Cannes Film Festival. Veronica, a gorgeous model, slinks down the red carpet entrance wearing 500 diamonds and little else. The gold body bracelet, in the shape of a serpent, was designed by Elli Medeiros for Chopard Jewelers. The total weight is 385 carats and with a built in security system, the piece is worth U.S. $10 million.

Before the screening, Veronica gets permission from her producer to go to the bathroom and we see she is accompanied by two moderately sized bodyguards, dressed in tuxedos. No muscle bound goons, we expect them to act as professional as they look. Alas, they make one mistake after another. They also have that bodyguard in a movie nervousness that drives me crazy and would make me even madder if I had to work with people like that in real life. The idea in real life is to make everything look easy, smooth, to be inwardly alert and aware of your surroundings but outwardly look very calm, cool and collected. In a situation like this you are on display as well.

Mistake # 1 Fail to provide proper coverage - Inside the Circle of Protection.

With two bodyguards covering $10 million in jewels, one should be on point, in front of Veronica, the other should follow behind. She would be in the center of the circle of protection. Instead the two bodyguards follow, look at the same things at the same time and do not appear to act like a team. We know right away they are not very good.

Mistake # 2 Fail to secure the room, the bathroom.

There is hardly anyone in the lobby, the film is about to start. There should be no one in the ladies toilet. Neither bodyguard thinks to check the "Femmes" before Veronica enters, and secure it for her and her $10 million dress. If one of the bodyguards was on point, he would have ducked into the bathroom first to clear it. I do this all the time when working with high level celebrities. What is the point of looking after them if you let them loose in an unknown space where anything can happen? You do not want to see on the web a photo or video of your Protectee peeing do you?

This is Secret Service 101. If you cannot clear a room, the Protectee does not enter, period. You always clear the room or space before the Protectee enters.

For such a high risk item, one bodyguard would clear the room, get anyone out and see that Veronica is safely alone inside, while the other stands guard directly outside, as in right outside the door.

Who would be embarrassed by a male bodyguard checking out a ladies toilet at Cannes? It's France! It would be more embarrassing to lose $10 million worth of diamonds in an unsecured space. The two bodyguards assumed the toilet was safe. How can you assume any space is secure unless you check it thoroughly? Which leads us to the next security leak. No pun intended.

Mistake # 3 Take a bathroom break at the wrong time.

One of the bodyguards leaves his post to go to the bathroom. In this business, especially when so much is at stake, you pee on your own time. You really need a strong bladder in this job and to watch your liquid intake.

Mistake # 4 Fail to use an unlocked stall.

This mistake follows from # 3, for it is really part of the same problem. When working armed, when you have to go, you use a locked stall. You never stand at a urinal with your pecker in your hand and a gun/knife/club in your pants. What happens if you are attacked or pushed? You are at your most vulnerable. This rule applies especially to nightclubs and of course any public bathroom. You are at your most vulnerable in a bathroom. You always use a locked stall, and so does your Protectee. I have been with a Protectee who goes to a bathroom in the nightclub with his entire entourage. Guys that is. It might sound funny in retrospect, but it is by far the most dangerous place as our French bodyguards find out. One in the Mens, one in the Ladies.

Mistake # 5 Fail to stop and question people who appear out of place.

This might sound obnoxious, but it is a good method of sorting out who is who in a new environment and you either make new friends or enemies, either way you filter out any possible threats.

The one remaining bodyguard looks at the sweating nervous engineer dressed in black, but never challenges or questions him as he walks past. The engineer has both hands closed, and appears out of place where everyone else is in formal dress. The encounter is questionable as many bodyguards would not talk to such a person. A "friendly stop and talk" is a professional way to screen such a person who "does not look right." Just glaring at the person, when there is no one else around, does not work. "Glaring" is for the wife when she sees you dressed in your favorite shirt that she hates.

To be professional, we stop and talk to anyone who appears out of place or who acts suspicious. For although we do not have arrest powers we do have the power of social interaction, the art of gentle verbal and tactical conversation and the ability to quickly assess a person based on their physical and verbal behavior. Acting friendly and engaging someone in small talk does not mean you are any less tough than you think you are, only smarter. This sort of action, the judicial use of micro encounters, separates the true professional from the mere amateur who has the outward appearance (shaved head, goatee and tattoos) but not the tactical communication skills.

Mistake # 6 Be easily distracted.

Because the bodyguard is not directly in front of the ladies toilet, he is easily distracted by the returning engineer who approaches and surprises him, from behind. When the bodyguard offers a light to the engineer, he misses his future nemesis sneaking into the ladies toilet.

Mistake # 7 Do not communicate or act with your partner.

The distracted bodyguard enters the bathroom once he receives the alarm. The other bodyguard is still a little under the weather having been zapped then placed in a stall. The bodyguard in the ladies bathroom acts so coy, on his best behavior as if he has never been in such a mysterious environment before. Entering any space where there could be a threat, you move in fast, ready to react immediately and you keep moving. You do not stop and offer yourself as a static target with your jacket buttoned. A stationary target is an easy target. In tactical firearms training you are taught to keep moving.

Mistake # 8 Keep your jacket buttoned up and stop in the fatal funnel!

The bodyguard finally unbuttons his tuxedo jacket. If you carry a gun whether it be in a waist level holster or a shoulder rig, you always have your jacket unbuttoned. If you have to sacrifice clean slim lines versus being tactically ready, choose broken lines, choose life. This dull guard still does not draw his gun.

Lets review the current situation for our bodyguard with the clean slim lines of a buttoned tuxedo. The jewelry alarm has gone off, he is entering an unsecured space with an unknown threat, without his partner, with whom he has no communication, and he still does not have his gun out, but look, finally he unbuttons his jacket. He does not understand that action is faster than reaction.

When you enter a room and there is a possible threat inside, do not stop in the doorway. This doorway is called the fatal funnel. You have to get through the doorway fast. It is the perfect place for an ambush. If there is a bad girl inside, she will be focused on this fatal funnel, the doorway. She will know where to aim. If you stay still, you give her a perfect opportunity to shoot you. Our hapless, soon to be eyeless bodyguard finds this out too late. It is so annoying seeing actors in action films or police procedurals stand in the doorway, clearly illuminated, a perfect target.

In training, you are taught to keep moving. You get out of the doorway and the light behind that makes you a fixed target. If you keep moving, you are less likely to get hit.

You cannot draw, aim and fire your gun if someone else already has you in her sights. He finds this out the hard way when he gets shot in the face with a dart. In a situation like this, if you have to draw your gun, it is already too late.

Look at any video or photographs of Secret Service agents in the winter protecting the President. They might be wearing heavy coats and a jacket underneath but their coats and jackets are both open. Their hands are at the ready. They do not have the time to unbutton anything if they have to draw their weapon. They can quickly draw down on any threat.

Mistake # 9 Fail to carry a flashlight if you work at night.

What tool will you always have a use for? And allows you to see and identify targets or threats in the dark? The flashlight is one of the single most important tools a bodyguard needs, all the time. If a new bodyguard shows up to work for me without a flashlight, and pen and notebook, I send them home to Mummy. They missed the briefing on what to always carry.

The power is cut to the building just as the photographer exits the bathroom with the bag of jewels and faces a bewildered second bodyguard. Everything goes dark and the bodyguard is helpless. The photographer escapes wearing her night vision goggles. She can see in the dark, the one surviving bodyguard cannot.

OK, so we have emergency lighting in the U.S. but still it can be too dim to properly make out what is going on in an emergency and nothing lights up a space like a 200 + lumens small flashlight.

Nine mistakes cost the client $10 million.

That is over a million dollars for each mistake. If this were real life, would the bodyguards have done any better? Despite the necessary plot points to advance the story and drop the viewer into an intriguing and unpredictable film, how the bodyguards behaved in the script demonstrated nine basic principles in protection.

1. Always enclose your Principal in a circle of protection.

2. Secure the room before the Principal enters, especially unknown toilets where she is carrying $10 million in diamonds, clear the room - it's a golden rule.

3. No bathroom breaks while you are working - and on high alert.

4. Always use a locked stall if you have to go to the bathroom and you are carrying weapons.

5. Stop and question any unknown people who enter your secure area, especially if they do not look like they belong. Being friendly and casual is equally disarming. Glaring at someone is just not professional, leave that to your wife or girlfriend, or both. You have to control the space around the Protectee. If someone enters that space, find out who they are. This can be accomplished with the minimum of fuss.

6. Do not be distracted. If someone tries to attract your attention, look around, be aware. Ask yourself why is he talking to me? What is going on here that I am missing? Have 360 degree awareness.

7. If you are working with a partner, stay in communication. Keep your partner informed of your position and act in concert with one another. You are a team. Always look out for your partner.

8. The jacket is always unbuttoned whether you are armed or unarmed. And do not stop in a doorway or the fatal funnel.

9. Always carry a flashlight, or two. A small powerful flashlight can fit into your pocket and you will use it far more than a handgun. You hope you never use your handgun, but wearing out batteries in your flashlight is good. Batteries are ultimately a lot cheaper than bullets. But first you need brains.

10. Do not believe anything you see in the movies. They are after all, only movies.

Chapter Twelve

The Best Bodyguard Jobs

The best bodyguard job is the one you have right now, where you are getting paid on time, are well fed, and you are part of a well drilled team. Or maybe you are on your own but have enough control over your security and your Protectee that you have a level of satisfaction that you have worked hard to achieve. You make it look so easy. Everyone is relaxed but aware. You can joke around in private and enjoy your bodyguard mates' company. The Protectee is not demanding but appreciative of your quiet professionalism and so are the people around him or her. You work for a small dynamic organization that cares for you and your bodyguard mates. There is a minimum of bureaucracy and you are self supervising. You want to be the best you can be and no one can stop you but yourself.

For every great bodyguard job there is the other side, a challenging client or Protectee, but like a nightmare, it does not last forever. But like a nightmare, it can repeat, over and over.

The Celebrity Nightmare

Maybe there are great celebrity bodyguard jobs. I know there are some fine actors, actresses and musicians who are a pleasure to protect.

But celebrities are a different matter. Some are famous for having no talent other than being famous. There lies the conundrum.

The Protectee is coming out of a nightclub, the back alley, the not so secret celebrity exit, not the so-called VIP entrance and exit where our SUV is parked and we have agreed would be the designated exit. We struggle to get the vehicle in position in the alley before the cameras arrive. The SUV with a hastily trained (read cheap and inexperienced) driver rushes up to her as she waits impatiently. She has been waiting for all of 30 seconds but it seems like an eternity as crowds begin to cluster around her and flashes start popping. And she is pissed and thinks we are not doing our job. This is true. We are not reading her mind. What mind? You ask. Exactly. And she is intoxicated, which only highlights our faults.

We get her into the vehicle but she slams the door before I can jump in and he zooms off. I run alongside. The driver has locked the doors; at least he learnt one lesson we taught him. I sprint alongside for the 6 blocks back to the hotel. Is this what Secret Service do with the Presidential limousine? In 90 plus degree heat and 100% humidity? I am soon drenched in sweat, and its only five minutes to midnight. I do not take the door slam personally. I am a bodyguard. I get treated badly at times and those types of jobs do not last forever.

Not one paparazzi managed to get an embarrassing photo of her snorting whatever she was consuming in the bathrooms she happened to be holed up in and lets not forget all the carrying on with another celebrity girl in a private party where they were sticking their tongues down each other's throats.

It's just another 18 hour day where two bodyguards keep up and protect an out of control celebrity. The good news is that shifts that seem like they will never end, eventually do end although your Protectee is taking stuff that you do not have access to, nor do you want to take, to keep them going and going and going.

One of the problems looking after young and not so young celebrities is the easy access to illegal drugs. How badly do you want to be part of that scene? This is one of the reasons why there is such a high turnover of bodyguards and their respective agencies amongst this type of clientele. I know well-respected bodyguard teams who have walked out on such bad behavior, out of control alcohol and drug consumption. Bodyguard agencies now write into their protection contract an immediate exit clause if the bodyguards become aware of illegal narcotic use or excessive alcohol abuse with their Protectee. When things go wrong, as they usually do with such drug addled celebrities, who do you think they will blame?

The universal rule is, blame the bodyguard.

The other side to this is, what happens when the celebrity does not hire bodyguards and a security driver?

The celebrity gets arrested.

Look at all the Driving Under the Influence (DUI) arrests, with out of control so-called celebrities. If they had only hired a bodyguard or a trained security driver, they would have avoided arrest. Drivers and bodyguards are cheaper than DUI lawyers.

What are the best Bodyguard jobs?

There are those amongst us who think the sweetest bodyguard jobs are full time salaried corporate protection details. But ask any bodyguard what their best job is and you will get different answers. There is a sense of being in history when you are protecting people in the public eye, public servants or elected officials or other persons under threat, real or imagined. Just handling the logistics of moving a large group of people from point A to B can be exhilarating and professionally fulfilling.

The best bodyguard jobs are the ones where you are treated with respect, are able to do your job without undue interference, work with great people and despite the long hours and endless shifts, get paid handsomely. No other job on this planet can give you the feeling that you have protected someone, made a difference, given someone peace of mind, not a piece of your mind, and excelled in your chosen profession. All of this takes place with little or no supervision. There is no bureaucracy or upper management to question or stifle your every move and initiative.

Is that too much to ask for?

The bodyguard job you could not imagine

"No teeth please"

I was in Las Vegas to look after the most downloaded amateur porn star in the world. Her manager had selected me after a series of grueling phone calls and now he was briefing me about my job in a penthouse suite that was next to my suite in a brand new Las Vegas hotel and casino.

"She likes to party at night and be with other women."

Okay, I nodded. Nothing to worry about there, I thought.

"But when they are down there, she doesn't like to be bitten. No teeth. Tongue is OK."

I hoped I did not turn bright red but I got the idea. No teeth. I fantasized, hovering over the naked squirming bodies of beautiful young women, if there was a referee hand sign for "No teeth!"

There are many types of bodyguard jobs from static posts in hotel corridors, or back alleyways next to back doors of private clubs, to running around just staying outside the lens of the paparazzi and your celebrity Protectee, or standing guard over an all female orgy.

The Way of the Bodyguard is rich in variety and challenges. There is the problem of complacency, being paid late or worse, not being paid, working with difficult clients and Protectees and working for and with other bodyguards who have different opinions about just about everything you can imagine.

A corporate bodyguard on the other hand can be an ideal long-term career. Looking after an executive, traveling with him or her and their families and living close by can be rewarding financially and professionally. Corporate protection can be boring, but boring is good in the bodyguard business.

Which reminds me, the Las Vegas porn star protection job also turned out to be unexciting but educational. There were no outrageous girl on girl encounters, no "No teeth please!" violations, but the hours were grueling and it was all business. I got to overhear multimillion deals being negotiated at 3 AM at a private party where men in worn T shirts were buying search engine words in multi-year contracts for millions of dollars. Every time you type in a dirty word or phrase in the top Search Engines, the traffic is directed to web sites these people own. They pay for these search words and phrases and in the early days of financial models for revenue on the internet, this was how Search Engines were being funded. No matter what content you offer on a web site, without traffic, without people clicking on your site, you do not stand a chance of making any money.

It is these moments, when you get glimpses of other worlds and how different business people operate, that makes being a bodyguard such an educational and eye-opening job. And we keep all this to ourselves. We do not gossip and we do not tell tales.

Here are some of the different types of protection jobs you might encounter.

Celebrity protection

Yes, there are wonderful famous people who are a pleasure to work for, do not demand 18 hour days for a 12 hour shift and they pay very well. These industry and entertainment icons keep the same bodyguards. There is a long list of such people and the bodyguards and teams who work for them. Vacancies do arise occasionally and these positions are highly prized.

Entertainment and film business people.

Running a security detail for a film crew or looking after an actress are specialty jobs. Every bodyguard job entails some type of specialty. There are the basics in security then there are specifics to that particular area. Being around famous actors who look so incredible on the big screen but in real life are small and ordinary, can be disconcerting. So can witnessing certain actresses in the nude. Then there is the adrenaline rush of trying to fight off hundreds of delirious fans as you usher your Protectee into a safe area.

Touring bands and performers.

There is nothing like the remorseless momentum of a long exhausting rock and roll tour. Current performers do not come anywhere near the excesses and out of control pandemonium of the glorious and drug fuelled anarchy of the previous late century rock and roll group theatrics. Touring today is still a tough job. Tour managers are better organized. Typically, they are not drug addicts, just territorial and obsessive. As they say in the touring business, it's not a sprint, it's a marathon, repeated over and over.

Single incident threat protection details.

These jobs can be the most interesting and the most dangerous. An out of control ex-boyfriend, ex-worker, ex-employee, ex-anything, makes explicit threats to an ordinary person who has never had any exposure to violence or bodyguard protection. That ordinary person is suddenly given a 24-hour bodyguard.

Witness protection.

U.S. Marshals are not the only ones tasked with protecting witnesses. Sometimes these jobs are contracted out to private protection agencies. There is a vast difference between a Law Enforcement officer who has no bodyguard training but has been on patrol for years and a highly trained bodyguard. But tell that to a patrol cop or a client who is happy with off duty untrained cops. Good luck.

Political or dignitary protection

What is the difference between a political campaign tour and a rock and roll tour? There must be a punch line in there somewhere. Viagra not Xanax? For a start, the groupies are older and heavier. Dress code, protocols, hours of work are a few differences that come to mind. Every protection specialty has its own dynamics and intricate behaviors; what is expected and what is not.

Stalkers, predators, threatening communications, embarrassing encounters and unwelcome visitors all have a way of creeping into the bodyguard's threat matrix, what a bodyguard can expect to encounter, especially when provided up to date intelligence and assessment from his office or support personnel.

Spending an enormous amount of time with a politician or dignitary certainly gives you an eye opening introduction to power, politics and persuasion.

There are other types of protection details.

Dealing with the mega wealthy is in itself a peculiar specialty. I say peculiar because if you were brought up poor working class or just plain middle class, dealing with the very rich is different. Different as in another universe different.

I worked for a woman who complained to me that she did not have the right color white slacks to wear when she is staring at a rack of 40 white slacks. What could I say to that?

Or the family that was paranoid about their own security but flew in their organic vegetables every day from the West Coast.

There was the couple who were so conservation minded that they recycled everything. They were very sensitive about their carbon footprint. They lived in a renovated double town house in Manhattan and flew their private jet every weekend to their massive compound in South Florida.

The Saudi Royal Family.

There are thousands of members of the Saudi Royal Family. There are four clans. They usually only marry amongst themselves. Visiting families to the U.S.A. seem to have more than their share of sickness and disability, which demands expensive medical attention from highly trained medical personnel, in exclusive medical facilities.

They pay in cash. There are vast quantities of cash in suitcases that seem to magically appear in diplomatic pouches. They love American movies, adventure theme parks, luxury hotels, shopping for designer clothes, buying expensive toys and eating and enjoying the freedom they can experience in the U.S.A.

But they still need protection from unwanted intruders, named and unnamed threats. In a sense, this is one of the most exciting and challenging bodyguards jobs. There are some great families to serve. It can be rewarding and an education in Bedouin and other Arab cultures. Accommodations are always first class. Would you rather sleep in a bunker or a five star hotel room?

And then there are the Logistics. With a capital "L," as in Love. You have to love the challenges that are thrown at you daily. Some you know, some you never see coming.

How do you tell a young woman who is calling from Paris with a one way First Class ticket to the U.S.A. that she cannot talk to her Prince? The horse handler, at least that was one of her positions, was not being allowed to board a flight to our city because she did not have a return ticket. It was 2 AM. I was talking to the First Class desk of this airline, but the call had been routed to India, so I was talking to a hysterical young woman in Paris on one hand and a wonderfully nuanced and melodious voice in Mumbai on the other. The horse handler cashed in her ticket for a return economy seat. She was unhappy but reaped the benefits of her travels later many times over.

How do you efficiently move 600 very large suitcases from one hotel to another when they are all black, unmarked or marked in Arabic? Of course their owners know which ones are their suitcases, but no one else does. How do you ensure all the oversized suitcases make it to the correct rooms and suites in the new hotel? How do you arrange for such a move, where 80 people expect to walk into their new rooms in their new hotel and have all their bags there?

There is a solution to the 600 giant black suitcases. Lists, labels, lots of help and making sure there are enough hotel staff briefed and ready to receive such a large shipment that usually arrives at some ungodly hour, early in the morning. The most important part though, is the envelopes stuffed with cash for all the hotel workers. If we arrive at the new hotel and all the workers get very fat envelopes, word spreads fast. We get excellent service throughout our stay.

How do you order another 747 cargo plane because the Family you are protecting bought so much stuff during their 3 month stay at a mid West city that they could not get everything into the 9 cans or containers that fitted below their other 747? Actually you just pick up the phone and talk to the family plane coordinator and order another plane. It was as easy as ordering a pizza.

How do you explain to the pilot of a specially chartered 747 with a crew of 12, that they are taking only one passenger back to the Kingdom? And he forgot his passport. It is in the hotel safe, two hours away. And while we are at the plane, can you take the Royal Hamsters. They are caged and no problem. In case you would not be able to sleep without the happy ending, the Prince did fly back to Riyadh, the only passenger. The pilot would not let the Royal Hamsters on board. (Thus you never got to see the horror movie "Hamsters on a Plane.") But there was a sad ending too. Back at the hotel someone forgot to feed the Hamsters and we discovered too late there was now only one. The female ate her mate.

How do you hire 50 new bodyguards in 48 hours because the General in charge of security decided at the last moment to fire all the locals in one city and only take his four favorite bodyguards to the next city? And you find this out when you are leaving in twenty minutes? The answer is you do not sleep for three days. Isn't this what you trained for?

How do you keep track of 60 drivers, whom you did not hire but are responsible for and need to communicate with, and 60 luxury cars and SUVs that have just been leased from multiple vendors? Spread over 5 hotels and 5 different bodyguard teams? We hired a car logistics person. We supplied her with a huge board, lots of pens, a radio, cell phone and a list of drivers. Throughout the detail we updated her on every car and driver movement that she kept track of on the board and on a large map, in our Command Post. The set up looked like a film set from World War II where all the bomber and fighter plane models are moved over a large map of Germany. We did not bomb Berlin but we did not bomb either. Unless you count the forgotten Suburbans.

How do you explain that three brand new black Suburbans have been left in the underground hotel parking lot for three months and no one knew they were there? The bodyguards were not blamed here, but an ambitious middleman was. He had been taking money from all sides and had forgotten to tell us about the extra cars he had rented for the Princes.

What do you do when a Filipino nurse, whom you have grown to like, wants to sneak out of her hotel room in the middle of the night and essentially escape from her contract? She has arranged to meet her family on the other side of town, even though her passport is being held by the General in charge of the security for the Family. And she knows she will be hunted down and sent back to the Kingdom, if caught.

What do you say to a young Sudanese woman who finally comes out of the Royal suite after being in there for over three months without leaving the hotel floor during that time? I said, "Hello, my name is Nick. I'm a bodyguard. If we can help in any way let me know." And I thought I had a tough job.

What do you say to the young Saudi sergeant in the Royal Guard who has caused the hotel's fire alarms to go into melt down? For the third time in a week, Fire and Rescue have come to his room to discover a burner on the carpet that he is using to heat his Hookah. That he nearly burned down the hotel and caused millions of dollars of damage and that the Fire Department is furious, somehow manages to escape him. The young sergeant does not care about the American firemen or the hotel management. He thinks he can do anything he wants because of who he is. Actually you appeal to his sense of pride and loyalty to the family he serves. Once he understands he will bring great shame to his superiors, the family that hired him, he gives up his electric burner. It took some persuading. Actually it took a lot of persuading. Little did the hotel management know that there were many other small electric burners hidden away in the rooms of the servants, so they could cook their rice at odd hours of the night. The servants could not call room service for themselves. They made their own meals in their tiny rooms.

What do you do when the 15 year old Princess is riding the elevators trying to pick up an NBA player at 2 AM. The hotel is one of the preferred hotels for touring NBA teams and she loves NBA players. We had a female bodyguard glued to her when the NBA was in town. She could still meet the players but she was always chaperoned in the hotel where her family thought she was safe.

What happens when the young Prince cannot do his English homework and comes to the Command Post and insists one of the bodyguards completes it for him. The trouble was finding a bodyguard smart enough to do the homework correctly!

The Saudi Royal family travels to particular places and hires mainly locals to supplement their own Royal Guards and a few chosen trusted bodyguards. It takes time to gain their trust and the respect of the people in charge of these families.

As in any culture, there is a full range of personalities and plots to make life interesting and no day is the same despite what appears like a boring routine amongst some of the family members.

Government leaders and politicians

The Secret Service looks after World Leaders, Presidents and Kings. The State Department's Diplomatic Security Office of Protection looks after other visiting ministers and dignitaries but there is plenty of work for private bodyguards for other leaders and dignitaries. Knowing their customs, how they operate and what they expect are vital. It is not the sort of job you can fall into. As with the Saudis, you have to know what you are doing and look like you know what you are doing.

Pharmaceutical Companies

If ever a single industry needed a lot of security, it would be the small number of heavily invested and all pervasive pharmaceutical companies. They bring new drugs to market after extensive testing and trials, not to mention the intricate and expensive Government approval process and they need protection. Protection from animal rights activists for out sourced animal and biological testing facilities, protection from industrial espionage or competitive intelligence as some refer to the game of spying on your competitors, and protection of the new drug launches. I have not mentioned counterfeiting and other fraudulent activities. Protecting brands and products is an entirely different side to corporate security and requires related bodyguard and investigator skills. But back to the protection side, such operations can be expensive and require a lot of bodyguards.

The sad reality is that very large companies like to talk to other very large companies, not some little local bodyguard agency. So what happens is one of the top people in a very large corporation will talk to the head of say a large security company and hire this security company at a very high price. We are talking several hundred dollars an hour. This transaction or decision-making process might take place on the golf course, the boardroom or over an expensive lunch. The Gigantic Security Company has lots of long expensive words in its mission statement and credentials, to describe its risk assessment and risk mitigation.

What actually happens is that the head of this Gigantic Security Company who is most likely a retired Federal Law Enforcement official or someone with similar stellar credentials (and who has been behind a desk for the last 10 to 15 years), talks to his head of security who then calls me or what could be worse, a friend of mine in another bodyguard agency who then calls me. What started out as a rather large sum per hour, similar to what top lawyers would charge, is now reduced to a very low two digit sum for yours truly who is actually doing all the work. I finish up not only doing the bodyguard work but providing the actual risk assessment and analysis, which of course I send over to the agency that subcontracted me, who in turn sends it to the main contractor, who in turn processes it, prints it in color with some pretty pictures, inserts some nicely placed very expensive words and presents this in a preprinted color brochure with their branded image to the client.

The entire process has happened many times. What makes the matter worse is that the local security head can turn around and ask me to work and be paid by them directly because he has figured out he can save his company so much money by cutting out all the middlemen. I have to point out I cannot do this. First, it is unethical. Second, I would destroy the trust between the primary agency and the agency I am working for, and so on down the line. And third, once you get a reputation for cutting out people and going directly to the source to get work, your reputation in this industry is shot. Loyalty means a lot, even for cut-rate sub-sub-contracted bodyguard jobs.

So later in the board room of the drug company:

"Skip, you know that former FBI hot shot you hired. They did a bang up job of the new launch." The CEO brandished a four-color security brochure.

"Bit expensive though. Almost $125,000!"

"But our earnings are projected at a million dollars a day with this new drug. We got a bargain." Skip replied.

"I see what you mean. Still, it was expensive, they charge attorneys rates."

"Have you seen our outsourced legal bills?"

"Still nothing happened, so maybe we don't need so much security next time."

One great benefit of working security for drug companies is the predictable work hours. The corporate executives do not go out at night to party at high-risk locations, such as gentlemen's clubs. Maybe it is because of the threat of blackmail from ever-watchful competitive intelligence companies, but they are very well behaved, go to bed early and work hard, the case for many, but not all, corporate protection jobs. If it is predictable structure and disciplined Protectees you want, being a bodyguard in corporate protection is a great career.

Jewelry Representative Protection

Not so with the average jewelry representative, one of the most dangerous and underpaid jobs out there. So many jewelry representatives are in denial over how many threats there are and how vulnerable they are carrying multi million dollar packages of jewels and precious gems. Hiring protection is a business decision that might be more influenced by lost profit from paying security rather than lost profit from someone stealing their jewels. There are far more losses in this business than are ever officially reported. Just as pharmaceutical company protection is a world unto itself, so is the jewelry representative world.

As in any high risk occupation, the biggest threat to jewelry representatives is their own hubris, their own sense of false security, complacency, that every day is just a series of routines.

Jewelry representatives are vulnerable to a variety of threats while traveling. The most ominous and violent threat is an organized group that specializes in stealing merchandise from the jewelry representative (we'll call them "reps" here). The FBI has identified a large number of people whom they call SAFGs, South American Theft Groups, who are highly trained and motivated.

SAFGs have defined territories in the U.S.A., travel on false passports and false nationalities. They are mostly Columbian, look like ordinary people, can blend in with their surroundings and half of them are women. They are either related or have some close connection to one another. If arrested, they do not talk. They do not even ask for a lawyer. They remain silent. They are well trained and mock our system of justice. They are hard to prosecute unless caught red handed. When deported, they reenter the country under another identity, wiser and more skilled. And start working again.

No matter what countries these groups come from, they are highly skilled predators, and can carefully select their victims, work out a plan of attack and accomplish their mission with minimal physical risk to themselves. But do not underestimate their ability to inflict violence to achieve their goal. They are also skilled in surveillance and counter surveillance techniques. This in turn could benefit a resourceful and vigilant bodyguard who can identify such surveillance, if the rep hires a bodyguard.

Predators select the weakest, not the strongest

Wildlife predators attack the weak, what we call soft targets. Any group of predators, whether they be hyenas, lionesses, or wolves, will select, after careful observation, a weak member of the group they are preying one. They do not select the strongest, they deliberately select the weakest, such as a young member unattended by its parents, an older animal not looked after by its siblings. The aim is a successful kill, a high yield with the minimum of risk or harm to the attackers.

Human predators operate on the same principles. They select the unprotected, the unaware, the weak. The traveling jewelry rep can be a perfect soft target. Put this individual in a new environment and the predators can close in and attack with the minimum of physical risk to themselves and an assured successful outcome. The rep can display a total lack of tactical awareness. He can be a creature of fixed routines, such as stopping every afternoon for cigarettes at a gas station between visits to his clients. He never checks his rear view mirror for any cars that might follow him. He never looks around when he parks. He parks in unsafe areas or pulls off the road to answer his cell phone or check his map or GPS. All these behaviors will attract the group who has selected this unfortunate rep. Such targeting is usually not random but based on previous research.

How not to be a victim

There are many security strategies reps can adopt, however, the predators already know these same tactics. The predator can tell that the rep is dressing down with casual clothing and that the tattered old bag the rep is carrying actually holds valuable merchandise. They have been surveilling this target for some time so these little ploys of the rep are laughable. Predators who work in organized groups can carefully select the time and place to attack their prey, and acquire the valuable merchandise.

What would stop such an experienced group from their predatory behavior? How can a rep deter such an attack? How can any jeweler stop such groups from selecting them as a target?

The answer is simple, although the execution is complex. The rep has to make himself a hard target.

Self defense or is it self medication?

Some self defense strategies that reps rely on can be likened to self medication for the drug abuser and alcoholic. They might make you feel good but they are worthless and ultimately very dangerous.

Do you travel with a firearm? If so when was the last time you fired it at a range? When was the last time you cleaned it? Can you draw and fire it safely from your seated position inside your vehicle? Do you know how to fire a pistol in a closed car?

Let us say you travel with a .38 snub nose revolver under your car seat. Now if you are held up at gunpoint, can you get to your firearm? If so, what can you do? Remember action is faster than reaction. If the predator already has a firearm aimed at your head, you cannot reach under the car seat and pull out your firearm in time. There are well documented cases of firearm owners being shot in their cars when they try to reach for their gun. And there are other considerations as well, such as the caliber of your pistol. A small caliber firearm might not penetrate the glass in the car, leaving you with shattered glass, blind to the outside and deaf from firing a gun in an enclosed space. Did you remember to keep your mouth open when you fired? Have you been trained to shoot from an enclosed vehicle?

So how can you make yourself a hard target? The solution is to hire a bodyguard who understands the jewelry business, how jewelry representatives work, and how jewelry thieves and predators operate. The ideal situation is to hire someone with the maturity and experience to work closely with the rep to ensure their safety and security.

A bodyguard should be able to closely oversee your travel, as well as devise a simple but formidable security plan.

The ideal jewelry bodyguard and security escort

What makes an ideal protection professional? Am I repeating myself here? Of course I am. Ask the people who work for me if I repeat myself. I will repeat the lesson until it is learned. We can call ourselves bodyguards or executive protection agents, but we need certain qualities that make us stand out and give the predators second and third thoughts about hitting their now hardened target.

What I look for in a bodyguard is maturity, alertness both physical and mental and integrity. I want an emotionally balanced individual who looks fit and physically imposing. I do not mean round as in apple shaped, or like a huge ex-club bouncer with a duck waddle walk. No, I mean a certain inner strength and fitness that projects confidence not arrogance. A quality that predators will pick up on and say: "I'm not messing with this guy. He might not look big but he looks like he knows what he's doing and we've come across guys like that before. Let's move on to our next target." We want the predators to move on to an unprotected easier victim.

The huge bodyguard with the big belly might look imposing but someone with a strong street sense can tell if such a person is a real threat or not. Perhaps one sharp kick to the knees and the big guy will crumble and all that fat will collapse onto the sidewalk in a screaming heap. Some of these large men with long goatees; perfectly shaven heads and really cool (they think) tattoos can fold rather quickly under extreme stress as in getting hit hard.

Next, I look for experience. I like bodyguards who have conducted a lot of investigations and interviews. They can be ex-Law Enforcement or private investigators but they will have a strong street sense, can read people and situations very quickly and have a very credible intuition regarding unknown people and possible threats. As for integrity, you cannot last in this business without it. You either have high moral principles or you do not.

It is the same with being alert and having good street instincts. You cannot conduct counter surveillance without having lived through thousands and thousands of hours of surveillance. A professional bodyguard needs to be well versed in counter surveillance and be able to look for tell tale signs that his Protectee is being watched. All those weeks and months sitting in a car looking at a door across the street certainly pays off, when you are a professional bodyguard. You can read a group of people, a street scene, any situation immediately, and know what is happening and more importantly, what is about to happen.

Do not underestimate the predator who is casing the rep. Despite a lack of formal education and perhaps an intellect that is challenged, predators can have finely honed street instincts and the ability to read people and situations in a manner a highly educated academic could not imagine.

There are as many types of bodyguard jobs as there are threats and challenges that bodyguards face.

There are other types of bodyguard jobs from factory closings and strike details with large groups to one-person protection details. There are Command Post positions where you are co-coordinating multiple bodyguard teams with a large group of Protectees and then there is that lone corridor position.

Command Posts are a world unto themselves. Take a hotel room, remove the beds and pictures and other furniture. Bring in tables, chairs, TVs, computers, video monitors for cameras placed in the hotel, notice boards, maps, other boards for schedules and contacts and you are on the way to creating a Command Post for the bodyguard detail that is operating in the hotel. There are radio chargers set up on the floor, wiring and wireless repeaters for the cameras that are monitoring key choke points and corridors on specific hotel floors. Then there is the new guy who is assigned to the corridor with the difficult Protectee who has fired the last three bodyguards he has encountered.

You are standing in that hotel corridor on your first day. You have met, very briefly, your Protectee and you are now waiting for him to appear at the door to be escorted down to his waiting car. You do not know if he has already called for his driver, or if the Protectee expects you to alert the driver. You do not know where the driver will be. In the garage or outside by valet parking? With quality training behind you and the ability to improvise and think fast on your feet, you are in for an exciting ride in your career as a bodyguard.

Chapter Thirteen

The Big Finish

I think the Agent only read the first page of my book and the last.

The Agent said:

"Don't you want to finish big? Don't you have an outrageous story? Some blood and guts instead of all this boring standing in hotel corridor stuff and going on about OODA cycles and having two flashlights and always carrying a knife and so on?"

Maybe he did read the book.

So I threw out my T.S. Eliot quote from the final line of "The Hollow Men," a perfect poem for modern bodyguards in the U.S.A.

The agent was not impressed.

"You are not suggesting that bodyguards whimper are you?" The agent asked.

"Really a bodyguard's job is to avoid and deflect any confrontations. As in,

This is the way my shift ends

Not with a bang but a sigh."

"If I was always getting into fights and last minute escapes, then I would have been doing a poor job as a bodyguard. Proper prior planning and all that."

"OK, but there has to be one story that you can close on that will leave the reader with a warm feeling."

We all have war stories. We tend to keep them to ourselves. Sometimes we do not come out looking so good. As in, why didn't you see that coming? If the Protectee was not harmed, embarrassed or was not aware of how bad the situation really was, it would be OK.

What is the big deal anyway with what happens to us late at night and away from any witnesses or cameras?

So some guy tries to attack us and he finishes up in the gutter. He is not dead, just a little shaken up and confused. We did not stop to check on him or his mates. What is the point of that? We did not kill or maim anyone. We just took care of the threat and that was that. Sometimes, most times, the Protectee was unaware of what had happened until much later. Take care of the threat, drop him and keep moving. There was no cell phone video, no CCTV footage. Nothing officially happened.

These little incidents are best underplayed. As I said, no big deal.

Then there are other stories, where the Protectee is definitely a participant in the process and maximum publicity, that is really bad publicity for our Protectee is the goal.

Do you remember the scene in the film Spinal Tap, where the band leaves their dressing room and tries to make it onto the stage in some mid-west arena? The crowd is screaming for them. We can hear the crowd. But the group, Spinal Tap, never makes it on stage. They get lost backstage, in the bowels of the arena.

That did not happen to the detail I was running. Although it was in the back of our minds, when we rehearsed our escape and evacuation plan. If you have been underground or behind the scenes at any large arena you will know how confusing it can be. Then add the noise and the sheer confusion of people running about the corridors and other temporary spaces, it can be even more disorienting.

As a bodyguard, you have a plan to get into a location. For a set appearance, for a performance at a certain time there is a choreographed arrival, screening and waiting process. Then you have to plan your departure. It could be a dignified and planned exit, what usually happens, under normal circumstances. Then you have to plan for extraordinary circumstances; escape and evacuation. (E&E). When something goes wrong, you have to get out of there fast, to protect the Protectee.

We had set arrival and rehearsal times for the live stage performance by our Protectee, for the special concert. Lets call it an Awards ceremony in a large arena, broadcast live to a worldwide audience. But this was not going to be just another Awards show. We started to collect street rumors, intelligence and other information from certain trusted sources about what was in store for our Protectee.

Someone had planned a hit on our Protectee after he had performed live on stage. There were two busloads of young men who had traveled from a certain nasty neighborhood. They were armed and had been given free tickets and back stage passes. They had been told that whoever "gets" our Protectee would receive a large sum of money. That made for about 100 people we would have to watch out for. We heard they would come in another entrance and would not be searched. They would be in seats near the stage our Protectee would be performing on and they would have backstage passes. We had come in through the main artist's entrance for the rehearsals and we were searched each time. We had to clear a magnetometer and so could not carry any weapons. That meant no knives, batons, clubs or guns.

The planned attack would happen out of view of the cameras but would create tremendous publicity with all the media present. The attack would also have bolstered the sponsor's bad guy image and sold more albums, more movie tickets. It was a huge investment for the alleged mastermind of the attack. This rival performer could only benefit from any violence created back stage.

We accompanied the Protectee and his performers, the entire entourage, to the two rehearsals. We picked up more whispers about what was planned. I guess if we were counter terrorist experts we would have called this "chatter." Some of these rumors, we could not verify, other pieces of information we could.

During the second rehearsal, we walked through the exit plan with the stage manager then we practiced the escape and evacuation plan five times on our own. The stage manager knew about the threat and advised us on our evacuation route. He also confirmed some of the "chatter" we had picked up. We firmed up our escape routes, mindful that when we returned later that night; our route would have changed in appearance. There would be less arena lighting back stage, more props, temporary barriers, people wandering about, a lot of noise and other distractions.

We ran through the escape plan one more time, almost blindfolded. I did not want to finish up lost back stage or worse, knifed and shot back stage.

The actual performance by our Protectee went as planned. The entire show was choreographed to the second.

Then, just as we expected, our attackers started to swarm the Protectee, as soon as he left the stage.

I had positioned myself out of camera range. I still had an excellent vantage point of the front of the stage and the backstage exits nearest to the stage he was performing on.

We were at an advantage because we knew the attack was coming, we knew who the attackers were, not individually, but as a group, and we had a sound escape and evacuation plan that we had rehearsed over and over again.

When I saw the attackers, I got him off the stage and onto our route out of the arena. I did not have time to count them but some of our party who were running as fast as they could behind us counted at least 50. The attackers seemed to be gaining on us.

I was on point but tried not to run. I walked quickly without appearing to be concerned. The Protectee was tripping over my heels and telling me to run faster.

We bundled him into our waiting SUV and the driver who had been told to drive off, floored the accelerator. A cop at the corner of the next intersection flagged him down.

"Is everything all right?" He asked. I stuck my head out of the window and smiled back and said yes, we were just a little excited to be leaving. The others were sweating and still hyperventilating. We had all grabbed our guns and we had kept them out of view.

The attack never had a chance to happen. We had gotten out of there as fast as we could, without the appearance, I hope, of running scared.

Back at the Protectee's home we found out that there were groups of these so-called attackers roaming the city, the after parties, the usual night clubs, looking for their target. Us. Someone was hoping to collect a large sum of money.

We stayed in that night. I had earned my night's fee for those 8 minutes of stage time performance and the long seconds it took to exit the arena.

Proper advance planning, solid intelligence gathering and analysis coupled with relentless rehearsals had prevented something deadly from happening. There was no bad publicity for our Protectee. I made a note to myself that I had to find another Protectee who was not a magnet for every thug who wanted to become infamous by attacking my client.

Adventures like this surpass the long hours in a hotel corridor waiting for an executive to come out of his suite. Adrenaline fueled events and endless shifts are all part of the Way of the Bodyguard. Looking back on your bodyguard career you can forget the tedium and the slow moving days and remember you kept your Protectees safe and secure. There is no higher calling.

Appendix A

Licensed Bodyguards in the U.S.

First, you have to be licensed

Licensing laws in States vary widely. Some States have no regulations. There are no Federal private investigator or bodyguard licenses.

Being a retired Law Enforcement officer under Federal Statute H.R. 218 (The Law Enforcement Officers Safety Act of 2004) does not necessarily give you a license to work as an armed investigator or bodyguard in particular States. As Henny Youngman could have said: "Take Florida. Please."

Licensing Bodyguards in Florida

The State of Florida recognizes bodyguards as investigators. To operate as a legal bodyguard in the State of Florida you have to have either a CC (intern) or C (private investigator) license, and be licensed as a private investigator. To be armed, you need to have a current G (State Firearms) License. You also have to work for an A (private investigator) agency and cannot be freelance. There is an exception for using a security guard with a D license for a temporary assignment, however, this is very temporary and the client is hiring a security guard to be a plainclothes (rather than uniformed) guard and this would apply to a B agency, a security guard agency. To those who own A agencies for private investigators, that is a big difference. A security guard in a suit is still only a security guard, even if the B agency is charging more for that guard's services.

If you are hired solely to protect one individual and you are on that individual or company's payroll and have no other bodyguard or investigation jobs you can do without the C and G licenses. Only the Concealed Weapon License (CWL) is needed. (You would need this anyway for carrying off duty if you had a G license.) But in an abundance of caution and knowing how legislation, enforcement and liability issues can change it would be wise to maintain a C and G license anyway, even if working under salary for one employee only.

Bodyguards come into this State and use the CWL loophole to work here. If you are a professional it is better to have a G License (higher standard) and be a private investigator. There is no mandatory insurance requirement now for an A agency. There are pitfalls to working under a CWL only. If you are caught in a bar, or a restaurant next to a bar or any licensed establishment that derives more than 50% of its revenue from alcohol you cannot carry with a CWL. You risk arrest and up to a $1000 fine from the Division of Licensing. Working with a C and G license ensures your legality and ability to work in places that would otherwise ban the carrying of firearms, excluding courthouses, Federal buildings and other security screened locations such as arenas. However you would already know where you would be able to carry because you would have performed your advance and know exactly where you would have to go and with what equipment.

Off duty or retired police officers who carry concealed legally under H.R. 218 still need to be licensed by the State of Florida to work as a bodyguard or armed investigator, and they need to work for an A agency and carry a CC or C license and G license. The same applies to out of state civilians who think that if they have a Concealed Firearm License they can work as an armed bodyguard, unlicensed in Florida. There are civil and criminal penalties for such violations. Well that is my interpretation of our State laws. But I am not an attorney. If you have concerns seek the appropriate legal advice.

The State of Florida has implemented reciprocity agreements with some States, however these can be confusing. Take California, PLEASE! To operate as an armed bodyguard in California, you need a separate guard registration card (whether in uniform or plainclothes - there is not the distinction that we have in Florida). You also need a permit for carrying an exposed Firearm, easy to get but not valid for use if you are plainclothes and do not have a Concealed Carry Permit. This is critical, the Concealed Carry Permit in California is difficult to obtain. You have to meet certain criteria, including being a California resident (a background check would reveal a California Drivers License and an address in the County where you are applying). You also have to demonstrate a specific need for a concealed firearm and get the approval from your local police chief who may or may not issue such a permit. If you are "just" a private investigator, you have a 30-day reciprocity agreement between California and Florida for strictly investigation work where the client and case originates from your home State. California has a separate private investigator license. If you are a bodyguard (plainclothes) and a private investigator in California you need two separate licenses.

Other States can be just as confusing. Every State that requires licensing has explanatory websites with information outlining how to acquire and maintain such licenses.

A quick search with your favorite search engine will reveal State specific requirements.

The Art of Bodyguard Networking

Make allies and friends

No matter how many licenses, how many certifications, how many top training classes you have attended, you are only as good as your network. Working with a wide range of body-guards you will be with some of the best and some of the worst. But remember if they are working and you want to work, you have to make allies. You will develop friendships based on long term bodyguard jobs where you have supported each other, shared the same room, and endured some of the same hardships and humiliations bodyguards quietly suffer in such details.

Appendix B

The Way of the Bodyguard Reading List

There are many great books to read relating to being a bodyguard. Then there are books that deal with what to expect from the other side, that is people who are trained to take out bodyguards and their Protectees.

This is my starter's list. There are more. The Way of the Bodyguard is full of new discoveries, new books, new instructors, new teachers, new ways of being a bodyguard, or at least new to me as I try to improve. There are books out there waiting to be discovered and devoured. Here are a few I have found be very beneficial.

1. Verbal Judo. Dr George L. Thompson and Jerry B Jenkins

   The Gentle Art of Persuasion

   I have referenced this text throughout this book. I have given away many copies. You should visit Dr. Thompson's website for more up to date information, classes and additional reading material. Check out http://www.verbaljudo.com/

2. The Gift of Fear and Other Survival Signals that Protect Us From Violence. Gavin De Becker.

   Mr. De Becker brings a different perspective to bodyguard work than the usual former cop or Special Forces operator. He runs a very successful protection and security business in Los Angeles. He has made a science of threat management based on personal and professional experience. He is a brilliant thinker and writer. If you only read one of his books this is the one, though there are several others you should read. Check him out here: http://www.gavindebecker.com/

3. Blink – The Power of Thinking without Thinking – Malcolm Gladwell

Bodyguards have to understand how decisions are made, fast. We live in an environment that we need to control or at least understand. If we can predict when rapid cognition takes place and realize why, we can act or react accordingly.

4. KGB Alpha Team Training Manual – How the Soviets trained for personal combat, assassination and subversion. Introduction by Jim Shortt.

It is not exactly the ex-Soviet Protection Bible but the manual shows how Russians thought, operated and accomplished their missions. How would you protect your client from such an operation?

If you really want to peek into the Russian Special Operators mindset read Viktor Suvorov's "SPETSNAZ –The Story behind the Soviet SAS." Suvorov, not his real name, was a Soviet GRU (Military Intelligence of the Soviet Army) defector with a wealth of information about how operators acted, thought and planned their missions, under Stalin and his successors. Some things never change and under the new Russian regime, we are witnessing a more sophisticated and a more efficient brutality. The way Russians think and operate on such security matters is vastly different from our American approach.

5. On the brighter side is Vladimir Vasiliev and Systema

Let Every Breath … Secrets of the Russian Breath Masters. Vladimir Vasiliev with Scott Meredith

An introduction to Systema and its secrets.

A secret until the early 1990's, Vladimir Vasiliev and Mikail Ryabko have made this system, this way of breathing, of living, of improving your self in all aspects including relaxing and fighting, available to the West. Systema is a revelation and a surprise, including the spiritual and psychological elements.

Here is a system we can use as bodyguards to control other people's bodies without being overtly aggressive or attracting attention to ourselves. This is not Aikido or Tai Chi or Wing Chung. It is common sense self defense using simple body mechanics, but with over a thousand years of experience in its applications. You have to see and feel these movements to understand how advanced and profound they are. The Systema seminar I attended with Maxim Frank was incredible. I came out of a very grueling workout feeling like I had been at a Yoga Ashram, meditating all day. That was how relaxed and euphoric I felt. Damn. Why didn't I know of this years ago when I was breaking wooden boards with a fully tensed body and shouting "Kaiiiii!" at the top of my lungs? The answer is, it was still a secret back then.

Maxim Frank will be the first to tell you that Systema is far more than just martial arts. Systema is breathing, posture, relaxation, movement and a lot more. It is a complete system and there is much to learn.

Vladimir Vasiliev as well as his mentor Mikhail Ryabko have released to the West, Systema and its secrets. If you have participated in any workshops with Systema practioners you realize how profound their way of thinking and their movements are as applied to body-guard work. Systema is performed relaxed, it is easy to use and very effective at close range. It is tactful and tactical in its use of the other person's body, whether it is one attacker or many. Systema has so much to offer.

Check out the DVD titled Personal Protection by Konstantin Komarov and Vladimir Vasiliev to see for yourself, how important Systema can be to your bodyguard skills and thinking. The Russian way is fundamentally different from Western approaches to protection and bodyguard work.

6. Principles of Personal Defense. Jeff Cooper

Our foremost authority on firearms and defense. A classic.

The Colonel was a prolific and profound writer. He redefined American gun fighting and made it what it is today. His "Principles" is a must read. When you have read Principles, you will want to read the rest of his no nonsense writings.

7. On Combat. The Psychology and Physiology of Deadly Conflict in War and Peace.

Lt. Col. Dave Grossman with Loren W. Christensen.

8. The Bulletproof Mind. Lt. Col. Dave Grossman

Lieutenant Colonel Dave Grossman has revolution-ized our thinking about fighting, killing and recovering from such trauma. If you attend one of his seminars, it will be a life-changing event. In the meantime, read his books. His website www.killology.com explains his re-search and writings.

9. Solo Training 1 & 2 The Martial Artist's Guide to Building the Core for Stronger Faster and More Effective Grappling, Kicking and Punching. Loren W. Christensen

There are many solo fitness books out there. Christensen, as a former cop brings valuable expertise into a mature and quick workout program. He makes great sense. You, however have to do the sweating. By the time you reach your 40's, it is no longer sensible to just do the occasional run or bike ride and lift lots of heavy weights. There is a more healthy injury free way of improving, not just maintaining your physical and mental well being and having the physical ability to work well into your 50's and 60's with a sensible work out regime.

10. KUDO Ancient Ways. Lessons in the Spiritual Life of the Warrior/Martial Artist. Kensho Furuya

There are many Zen inspired warrior books for those who identify with the samurai spirit or at least the idealized Western style version we celebrate today. Kensho Furuya brings a different perspective to martial arts.

11. The 47 Ronin Story. John Allyn

I had to throw this one in as it succinctly tells the most famous story in Japan of the 47 Ronin. If you understand this story, you understand samurai and therefore Japan. Too sweeping a statement? Of course it is. What would 47 bodyguards, sworn to protect their master, do in a situation like this? Would this happen now in the Western World? No, of course not. There would be 47 different real life confession books and film deals.

12. The Book of Five Rings. Miyamoto Musashi

    Translation by William Scott Wilson

    Musashi is supposed to define the samurai spirit yet he was atypical of any contemporary samurai. Long a recommended read for corporate executives intent on advancing in the brutal world of business, the text is beautifully translated by William Scott Wilson who really understands the culture. The text is a meditation on what it means to be a samurai. It is part of the Way. Also released is a graphic version of the Five Rings.

13. The Book of Five Rings: A Graphic Novel, from the book by Miyamoto Musashi, adapted by Sean Michael Wilson, illustrated by Chie Kutsuwada and based on the translation by William Scott Wilson.

14. Hagakure: The Code of the Warrior (The Manga Edition). From the book by Yamamoto Tsunetomo, adapted by Sean Michael Wilson, illustrated by Chie Kutsuwada and based on the translation by William Scott Wilson.

15. The Narrow Road to the Deep North. Matsuo Basho

    Readers might think I was influenced by Musashi to name the title of this book The Way of the Bodyguard. But my first influence and Japan's greatest poet was Basho and I have read The Narrow Road to the Deep North many times together with:

16. Zen Flesh, Zen Bones, a collection of Zen and pre-Zen writings, including Ten Bulls. Compiled by Paul Reps

    I have carried the same paperback across four continents. It's a little worn, like me. But the stories still carry surprises and insights.

17. The Unfettered Mind, Writings from a Zen Master to a Master Swordsman. Takuan Soho, also beautifully translated by William Scott Wilson

18. Musashi. Eiji Yoshikawa

This great novel started out as a serialized newspaper story published in Japan in the early 1940's. Over 900 pages and a great read. It is a sobering thought to realize this story was being read hot off the presses by a nation at war with the Allies. It is even more disturbing to realize these same young men were charging with their samurai swords, their katanas, held high at my father deep in the Burma jungle. My father had a large collection of katanas he had picked up in the mornings after these waves of suicide charges.

19. The Fifth Profession. David Morrell

The bestselling novel illustrates in dramatic form what a mess a bodyguard can get into. If you type in the word "bodyguard" in Amazon or use any other book search you will come up with a pile of steamy bodyguard romances. I included this novel (there is no bodice ripping in this one but there is some romance, more sweaty than steamy) because I referred to it earlier when I made a counter claim that bodyguards were the first profession, in the strictest biblical sense not the fifth profession. The Way is not to be confused with the other "First Profession."

20. Violent Encounters: A Study of Felonious Assaults on Our Nation's Law Enforcement Officers. The 180-page research summary is the third in a series of long investigations into fatal and nonfatal attacks on police officers, written by the FBI team of Dr. Anthony Pinizzotto, clinical forensic psychologist, and Ed Davis, criminal investigative instructor, both with the

Bureau's Behavioral Science Unit, and Charles Miller III, coordinator of the LEOs Killed and Assaulted program. The research and conclusions are very sobering and reinforces how important officer presence, read here bodyguard presence, can be in certain evolving violent situations. Their ground breaking research is must reading for bodyguards who want to understand what they are up against in the real world of psychopaths, killers and other deadly threats.

Force Science Institute studies how humans behave in stressful and violent encounters. Their research and scientific findings are a treasure trove of information related to Law Enforcement and security incidents that turned violent and chaotic. Their web site forcescience.org outlines many accessible articles and research projects and videos that demonstrate how to survive a violent encounter. If you have experienced such violent encounters, even in training, you will have lots of "Aha!" moments reviewing this material.

21. The Bodyguard's Story: Diana, the Crash, and the Sole Survivor. Trevor Rees-Jones, Moira Johnston

Princess Diana Final Crash Inquiry Report. Lord Stevens, 2006, Operation Paget. http://en.wikipedia.org/wiki/Operation_Paget

Trevor Rees-Jones explains what happened and then the Lord Stevens' Report exhaustively chronicles the unfortunate chain of events.

Other Fiction

There are former Special Forces operators, former intelligence officers, former bodyguards who have written compelling fiction, or as some claim, real life dramas, spiced up a little with the names and dates changed but still very realistic.

There is a huge difference in authenticity between someone who has done this type of work and writes about it compared to a journalist or writer who has just researched and interviewed people about this type of life, this type of mentality.

When it comes to violent encounters, there is no substitute for real life experience. If you have survived deadly situations, your attitude towards reading about similar experiences changes.

Lt. Col. Dave Grossman makes the analogy that it is like a virgin writing about sex, all theory and no practice. If you have not experienced combat and extremely stressful and violent situations, you cannot write about it accurately. Do not misunderstand me, to be a bodyguard you have to understand the psychology of violence, but you do not have to kill. Lt. Col. Grossman states, when the proverbial merde (that is French for shit, for the uneducated) hits the fan: "You do not rise to the occasion, you sink to the level of your training."

I have included a very short list of some of these writers here. There are others I have yet to discover.

Andy McNab

Andy is not his real name but he has made a well-deserved career for himself after surviving an SAS drop into Iraq during the first Iraq War. His fiction features a gritty working class lad, Nick Stone, who has retired from SAS but still works for the UK Government as an expendable and deniable operator. His tradecraft, endurance, improvisational planning and willpower are exemplary as is his self-deprecating humor.

Chris Ryan

Another SAS operator using a nom de guerre who was in the same unit in Iraq as Andy McNab and who is also a best selling author and TV personality. He has written a series of action packed and very realistic thrillers based on ex-SAS operators trying to make it in the real world.

Richard Marcinko

Marcinko is the SEAL who wrote the original Rogue Warrior series. In another country he would have been knighted, (U.K.) or made President (Israel), but in the U.S.A. he was sent to Federal Prison. He is very much alive and well respected in the counter terrorism community, and he writes superb fiction that blends outrageous story lines with realistic action sequences. A dire friend of Mr. Murphy and an avid admirer of bloody minded will power, revenge and superior fire power, some of his descriptions of purported top secret operations and procedures have rattled more than a few power players in Washington. He also makes enemies easily as was evidenced by his short Federal prison vacation. This has not hampered his booming security and consultancy business. He continues to write gripping stories that predict rather than echo future headlines. Call these books Special Forces Procedurals, they still provide an underpinning of surveillance and counter-surveillance techniques and a can do way of thinking that is perversely creative, downright twisted, blood-thirsty and very entertaining. Plus he always manages to procure the latest deadly toys and use them to stunning effect. I look forward to every new Marcinko novel, the witty writing, the plot lines and the sheer authenticity he brings to modern day terrorist hunting mayhem.

Barry Eisler

He only worked for the CIA for a few short years but the John Rain novels demonstrate in-depth surveillance and counter surveillance skills and an entire encyclopedia of assassination techniques wrapped in tight suspenseful writing. John Rain, the central character, exhibits tradecraft to die for. To get into John Rain's mind is a superb training tool for bodyguards. We all hope we never have to encounter such a skilled and unpredictable assassin. How can we train for something if we do not know what to expect? We train for the unknown threat, the hidden attack, the unexpected encounter.

John Rain stands as a deadly example we can all learn from.

After *The Way Of The Bodyguard*

After writing this book I graduated, not retired, from being a bodyguard to a full time investigator. I say graduated because everything I experienced and learned in the protection business, all the skills I acquired and the situations I got into and out of, I now apply as an investigator. What does that mean? It means I get to sleep in my own bed and see the wife every night. I am no longer tethered to a Protectee although I am very mindful of my own protection and keep my own counsel regarding personal safety.

The street interviews, call them field interviews, those chance encounters and small conversations with untrusting strangers help advance my investigations. I am overworked, underpaid, lacking in resources and have too many impossible deadlines, but who would have it any other way? I was describing this to an old friend, a Marine, and he just smiled and said, sounds like being a Marine. That was a real compliment and an inspiration.

There came a time when my wife wanted me home to look after her. Time to bodyguard the family and spend more time with those I love. No more seven-month long details in a distant location, with no breaks and no trips home, and 12 to 16 hour day schedules.

Those jobs are open to you if you choose the Way of the Bodyguard. The hours are long; the jobs can be tedious and endless. The Protectees and clients can be challenging. But the ultimate reward is protecting the threatened, the innocent and the anonymous.

The Way of the Bodyguard is a journey, not a destination. What is important is that as I walk in the shadows of another street in a crime ridden neighborhood, I am mindful of all that I have learned, forgotten and hopefully remembered again and written about in The Way of the Bodyguard.

I trust you have learned from my experience and writing. Now it is your turn.

After Thought For The Literary Agent

"What is The Way of the Bodyguard about?" The literary agent asked.

"To become a bodyguard, it's unlike any other job. As first mentioned in the Old Testament, it is the oldest and the most dangerous profession, with great rewards.

"To follow The Way of the Bodyguard in the Twenty First Century, means you have to make an extraordinary commitment.

"This book, The Way of the Bodyguard, is about that journey.

"It's a how to book. How to be a bodyguard and protect your client."

"Is that it?" The agent was unimpressed. "You need celebrities, embarrassing incidents, perilous situations, indecent revelations. Your readers want to know what rich and famous people get up to when no one is watching but the bodyguards."

The agent went on to say I would never sell any books if I did not tell these stories.

I replied that is not what this book is about. It's called The Way of the Bodyguard, not The Way of the Big Bald Badass Bodyguard who sells out and tells tall stories.

"It's not a kiss and tell memoir or a punch and kick confessional."

"Then who's going to read it?"

"Bodyguards. People who are curious about what it is like to be a bodyguard. People who want to become a bodyguard and those who dream of becoming a bodyguard. We all must dream. And some of us are destined to protect.

"This book is about knowledge, not gossip."

Acknowledgements

The Way of the Bodyguard would not have been written without a lot of help from a lot of people.

I want to thank all the bodyguards I have worked with or encountered. For all the security directors, Protectees and clients who hired me, I am indebted.

We, and I speak for a lot of bodyguards here, are always comparing ourselves to others in our profession as in, what does he know and have that I do not? What can I learn from him or her? I have often been struck by bodyguards who have a quality, a presence or skill that I could not possibly possess or master. There are some amazingly talented bodyguards out there who put me to shame. I have never said I am God's gift to bodyguards or that I am that good. I just have a good work ethic.

I am indebted to Robert Groom. He passed in 2010 of cancer but whenever I was working with him, I felt safe. And I had a great time. There are not that many men you can label "a Man's Man." He was that man and a whole lot more. We went shooting a few days before he died and he still out shot me.

A big thank you to Joe Biundini and Mark Trower, for working with me and putting up with me for so long, and to Eric Dybing for his courage and chutzpah.

I have to especially thank Adam Hamon from Regiment Security LLC, Ed Wilson, Shay Ben David, Brian Leek, Rick Norris and Wayne Black. Victor Reinosa taught me there is more to street sense than street. Despite his clients, I always felt safe working with him even when our radios did not work and we were outnumbered and outgunned in noisy chaotic situations. Shawn Wilson also exemplifies smart professionalism, especially with jewelry representatives. There are many more bodyguards I have worked with and I am missing out quite a few names. For this I apologize, or maybe I am respecting your privacy and sense of quiet professionalism.

Other bodyguards who have influenced me and I have learned from include Alex Lopez, Max Solon, Tony Volonino, Alon Nadler, Debra Conrad, Derek Signorelli and Mark Cahill. A special big thank you to Tom Curley, who showed me Marines make great bodyguards, provided they do not break any of our equipment.

Not to be underestimated with his wealth of training expertise and sheer good humor is Wally Philbrick. His classmate from police academy, Paul Lupien, provided me with a great role model in Law Enforcement. Paul taught me the importance of micro encounters and how very small gestures can be so important when interacting with the public. I learned the hard way never to go running with him.

Talking of extremes there is Art Lihte, my original Sensei who taught me you can never be too well prepared or armed. He demonstrated, in real life, why a 8th Dan (at the time) black belt with knuckles the size of oranges should still wear a full size 9 mm Berretta in an ankle holster and use it to good effect.

He made the mantra "You have no friends. Pain is your friend" come true in every session with him.

Later, I came across another extremely talented Sifu whom I will call Page. She had the most powerful legs I have ever seen and is a master at Chen style Tai Chi. Her soft, slow style was remarkable for its deceptive power and speed.

Talking of torture. You have not trained until you have endured one of Mirza David's bodyguard training seminars, whether in Europe or Israel. Mirza operates International Security Academy from Herzliya in Israel. He has trained hundreds and hundreds of extremely proficient and physically and mentally fit young men and women who have become well employed VIP protection specialists. (Don't ask, he does not like the term bodyguard and I would not argue with him!) His web site provides extensive details on his training and networks: http://www.securityacademy.com. I have fond memories of carrying steroid induced Berlin bouncers up little hills in the Swiss Alps and wondering if SEAL Hell week would have been easier.

Only after I met Bram Frank in 2000 did I realize you did not have to pummel someone senseless or get tortured to train properly. Bram's modular blade work and inspired teaching has changed the entire knife self defense community and injected a deep sense of realism into common sense self defense with edged weapons. Bram's book: Conceptual Modern Arnis: Filipino Martial Art, the art of Professor Remy Presas as seen by Bram Frank, contains lifetimes of learning. By lifetimes, I mean how Modern Arnis has absorbed and reinvented a wide variety of fighting and self-defense styles from medieval European sword and dagger work and the supremacy of Conquistadors in the fighting arts to Indian and Far East disciplines to Chinese and Japanese martial arts. Grandmaster Bram Frank is one of the World's Martial Arts living treasures and his use of the Gunting and CRMIPT (Close Range Medium Impact Tool) is exemplary (or should I say mandatory?) for bodyguard close protection work. You will want to keep a copy of his book by your bedside. And watch out for Sonia Waring as well, his protégé.

Bram Frank is one of the instructors at the S2 Institute in Clearwater Florida. Tim O'Rourke, the Director of the S2 Institute has done an enormous amount of work in creating a professional elite in Security, Bodyguard work and Investigations in Florida. His training facility and on line learning academy has broken new ground in disseminating knowledge in our profession and related disciplines. Tim is also a great firearms teacher.

J. J. Kelly, former Director of Lethal Force for the Miami-Dade Police Department and a decorated police officer, taught me how to shoot or I should say, shoot and move. Because his teaching knowledge is based on a lifetime of real life shooting and crime fighting, he stands in a class on his own when it comes to demonstrating skills, tactics and a winning mindset.

Every Systema instructor I have come into contact with has opened my eyes, improved my body and blown my mind. I include Maxim Frank, Frank Arias, Joe Gehr and the Merrell brothers. There are many more instructors I have not mentioned or have yet to discover.

There is a chapter in Yoshikawa's epic novel Musashi, that describes a sword polishing shop that has a sign that reads, "Souls Polished". A modern day grandmaster, who is a polished soul is James Williams. You can read more about James Williams and his System of Strategy at http://www.systemof-strategy.com/. He combines pre-twentieth century samurai skills with Russian Systema and other dark arts. He is much in demand from our military and other operators with no names or ranks. When you watch him on You Tube there is so much to miss, so much to learn. His movements look so simple, deceptive, hidden. Training in person opens doors into these movements. An opportunity to train with Mr. Williams is not to be missed. He has an enormous amount of knowledge to pass on.

Rabbi Pinchas Weberman inspired me to rethink how I work with bodyguards. His talks are always a revelation and have made me realize the Way can take many paths, many directions but still be the same journey. Rabbi Weberman's actions, writings and talks are always an inspiration and officers in the Miami Beach Police Department are more the wiser for having him as their chaplain and reserve police officer.

Special thanks to Lyn Kraft for lending her body for the cover photo, and to Toby Spill for looking more like a bodyguard than most bodyguards.

About the Author

My parents were Cockneys. I was born in Essex, England and emigrated to New Zealand in the 1960s.

I grew up in New Zealand, graduated from the University of Auckland and trained to be a primary school teacher.

I worked for the National Art Gallery and the Ministry of Internal Affairs.

During the 1970s, I took photographs and was a conceptual and performance artist.

The New Zealand Government awarded me an arts grant with a one-way ticket to New York, and told me not to return.

My first adventure in America was rescuing the wife of a Navy SEAL in Mexico. My original aim had been to study the paranormal, not the psychotic. Out of that escapade came the short story "Dolphin Kicks and Cactus Pricks."

In New York, I met and befriended an extraordinary man. An artist and lawyer who was a cross between Marcel Proust and Freddie Mercury, Gary was completely outside my ordinary frame of reference. He died young from what was then an unnamed epidemic. His story became "The Palace in TriBeCa."

I traveled extensively in the United States and worked in the rapidly changing world of computer and telephone integration, that eventually developed into the Internet.

In the mid-80's I moved to Miami Beach and as a consultant, I solved other people's problems.

After forming a Private Investigation Agency, I worked as an investigator and bodyguard to the rich, the famous and the anonymous.

I wrote "The Way of the Bodyguard" to give back to the Protection Industry.

Other Books by Nick Spill

Dolphin Kicks and Cactus Pricks (Kindle Edition) 99 cents

I traveled with a group of Californian psychics to swim with dolphins in the Sea of Cortez.

Instead I witnessed the psychics turn psychotic. I barely managed to escape Mexico with the wife of a Navy SEAL, a Greenpeace activist and a hippie left over from Haight-Ashbury.

The Palace in TriBeCa (Kindle Edition) 99 cents

In New York City I met and befriended an extraordinary man. An artist and lawyer who was a cross between Marcel Proust and Freddie Mercury, Gary was completely outside my ordinary frame of reference. He died young from what was then an unnamed epidemic. His story became "The Palace in TriBeCa".

Growing Up Horny in New Zealand (Kindle Edition) $2.99

A coming of age mock-u-memoir set in '60s and '70's New Zealand.

Growing Up Horny in New Zealand is a story of Nicholas Laurent who emigrates from bleak pre-Rolling Stones 60's England to New Zealand. In pursuit of girls, the young man seeks intimacy while failing to understand the fairer sex. This mock-u-memoir chronicles his journey from tragedy to comedy, from bedroom to art gallery, as Nicholas seeks liberation from the relationships that haunt his failed quest for nirvana.

Reluctant Q

By George Spill and Nick Spill

The quartermaster's tale of survival in the Burma Jungle in WWII.

George Spill was conscripted into the British Army at the age of 30. He was sent to India in the Royal Artillery and finished up in the Burma jungle. He fought through some of the most savage battles of World War II. He became the Battery Quartermaster and was one of the few who survived against impossible odds from the forgotten 14th Army. A reluctant war hero, this is his uncensored story.

Available as a Kindle edition for $4.95 and paperback $9.95.

Printed in Great Britain
by Amazon